D0914628

LEGAL ASPECTS OF
SCHOOL BOARD OPERATION

ROBERT R. HAMILTON

Dean, College of Law, University of Wyoming

E. EDMUND REUTTER, JR.

Professor of Education, Teachers College, Columbia

BUREAU OF PUBLICATIONS • TEACHERS COLLEGE
COLUMBIA UNIVERSITY • NEW YORK • 1958

INTRODUCTION

The local school board is a unique structural feature of education in the United States. Well over two hundred thousand citizens comprise the approximately fifty thousand bodies responsible for public education in their respective districts. Nine out of ten members of local boards are elected directly by the voters of the district. The others are appointed by individuals or groups popularly elected, such as the mayor and town council.

Certainly those who serve on school boards, or contemplate doing so, must be aware of the law as it pertains to local school operation. If they are not, the result at best is impaired efficiency; at worst, it is serious legal entanglements.

But anyone concerned in any way with the schools should be alert to the basic legal rights, duties, privileges, and responsibilities entailed in the public school enterprise. The stake in good public education of school administrators, teachers and other employees, parents, and citizens-at-large is so great and so dependent on legal considerations that a general knowledge of this field is essential.

It is the purpose of this volume to present the minimum essentials of the legal aspects of local school operation in such a way that the reader will be able to get both a general feeling for the process of the law as it affects education and also certain important specific information. Obviously the material that follows is selective. The bases of selection have been primarily importance of the items to local school operation and general applicability of the principles discussed. The frame of reference is that of the powers of the local school board. This approach, while encompassing the many areas covered by the chapter titles, necessarily causes some important legal concerns to be treated only briefly or not at all.

This volume presents the law as it is. The authors have endeavored to analyze and synthesize judicial interpretations of constitutions, statutes, rules and regulations, and the common law in an objective manner. Personal value judgments, legal or educational, have been avoided. Copious use is made of quotations from judicial decisions in the belief that much can be lost in paraphrasing as regards both flavor and accuracy.

Generalizations are made on the basis of a thorough study of all pertinent cases. The citations given are to those cases which seem best to substantiate points made. In this connection, it should be noted that in some instances an older case is cited in preference to more recent ones because the older case established the precedent which has been followed and more recent cases have cited the prior decision as controlling. Other criteria used in selection of cases cited were completeness and clarity of the court's opinion directly on the issue in controversy.

In connection with statements of rules of law, the admonition of Oliver Wendell Holmes to the effect that general propositions do not decide concrete cases must be borne in mind. At the same time, however, it should be realized that there can be no intelligent approach to a problem without examining it in the light of various competing general legal considerations. Such principles form a necessary background for examination of specifics.

Obviously no book can give detailed and irrefutable answers to all the legal questions in all the school districts. Variations in material facts of cases or in the laws of different jurisdictions may mean that some issues discussed would not be settled in the present jurisdiction of the reader as they were in the cases cited. There are, of course, many decisions of the Supreme Court of the United States which would prevail regardless of one's local situation and many common law principles which are likely to control in the absence of statutes specifically to the contrary. In addition, the manner in which courts have construed a legal provision in one state, while not binding on the courts of another state, may be persuasive.

The reader must keep in mind that this volume is intended only as a general orientation to legal aspects of local school board operation. It may help the legal layman to communicate more effectively with lawyers; it certainly is not a substitute for legal counsel. Remember: "He who serves as his own lawyer has a fool for a client!"

Robert R. Hamilton

E. Edmund Reutter, Jr.

CONTENTS

LEGAL ASPECTS OF
SCHOOL BOARD OPERATION

I

THE LOCAL SCHOOL BOARD IN THE
LEGAL STRUCTURE

EDUCATION AND THE UNITED STATES CONSTITUTION

The concept that provision for education is a state, rather than a federal, function evolves directly from the Tenth Amendment to the Constitution of the United States. That amendment reads: "The powers not delegated to the United States by the Constitution, nor prohibited by it to the States, are reserved to the States respectively, or to the people." Since education is not directly mentioned in the Constitution, power over it resides in the states. This does not mean, however, that the federal level of government is unimportant in relation to the legal aspects of school operation.

As will become apparent in subsequent chapters, the federal Constitution is directly applicable to a rapidly increasing number of legal actions involving local school districts. The First Amendment, as made applicable to the states by United States Supreme Court interpretation of the Fourteenth, bars any "law respecting an establishment of religion, or prohibiting the free exercise thereof." This provision has been the basis of much litigation regarding such diverse issues as Bible-reading in opening exercises, released time for religious instruction, non-participation of pupils in school activities for religious reasons, dismissal of teachers for being conscientious objectors to war, use of public funds to transport children to parochial schools, and use of school buildings for meetings sponsored by religious groups.

The Fourteenth Amendment has been the basis of many cases pertaining to public education in such situations as assignment of pupils to schools on the basis of race, loyalty oaths for teachers, and prohibitions against teaching certain subjects. The clause in the Constitution proscribing impairment of obligations of contracts is basic in the varied problems related to contracts with employed personnel and with outside persons or companies such as architects, building contractors, bus companies, and suppliers of materials. More recently the right extended by the Fifth Amendment against self-incrimination has been cited frequently in cases involving teachers. Federal legislation of direct concern to local boards pertains to such items as school lunches, vocational education, and social security.

EDUCATION AS A STATE FUNCTION

The constitutions of the individual states provide with varying degrees of specificity for the establishment and maintenance of systems of public schools. To implement these constitutional provisions, state legislatures have enacted statutes covering various aspects of school operation. The power of the state legislature over public education is plenary or complete, except as restricted by the state or federal constitution. In other words, the state legislature can take any action regarding schools not expressly barred to it.

In one of the leading cases in the area, the Supreme Court of Indiana described the legal power of the legislature regarding education as follows:

> The authority over schools and school affairs . . . is a central power, residing in the legislature of the state. It is for the law-making power to determine whether the authority shall be exercised by a state board of education, or distributed to county, township, or city organizations throughout the state. . . .

> As the power over schools is a legislative one, it is not exhausted by exercise. The legislature, having tried one plan, is not precluded from trying another. It has a complete choice of methods, and may change its plans as often as it deems necessary or expedient. . . .[1]*

To accomplish the ends expressed in state constitutions for public education, legislatures of the various states have set up local school districts.

* Cases cited are listed at the ends of chapters.

The bases of establishing districts or altering their boundaries vary, but it is clear that the legislature has the authority to create and alter districts. It may or may not assign to them the same boundaries as municipal units of government. It may classify them on reasonable bases, such as population, for the operation of various laws. Thus, within a state, school districts may vary in regard to such matters as method of selection of board members, arrangements for financing schools, mandated staff personnel policies, and even powers of local boards.

A school district legally is an agent of the state, responsible for the state function of public school education within a geographical boundary. Thus the district is completely subject to the control of the state. It sometimes is referred to as a special function unit, as distinguished from general function units such as counties and cities. Generally it is considered a quasi-municipal corporation, because while it has many of the characteristics of incorporated local government bodies such as cities, its powers are more restricted because its only function is in relation to education. A typical statement on the point is found in the following statement by the Supreme Court of Pennsylvania:

> While a school district is not, of course, an independent sovereignty, it does constitute a body corporate, a quasi-municipal corporation, which is an agency of the Commonwealth for the performance of prescribed governmental functions, being created and maintained for the sole purpose of administering the Commonwealth's system of public education. . . .[2]

It follows from the concept of education as a state function that school board members are state officers, as distinguished from local government officers. This is true regardless of how school board members are selected and regardless of whether school district boundaries coincide with municipal boundaries. In a leading case involving the right of a state to require that a local government unit levy and collect taxes for the support of public schools, the issue was discussed by the Court of Appeals of Kentucky in the following language:

> If the public schools of . . . [a city] were local affairs, over which that municipality had the sole control, it may be doubted if it would be competent for the state to levy a tax on its other citizens to help support them. But they are not municipal institutions at all. . . . The city schools, including high schools, are part of the state's common school system. Their trustees are officers of the state.[3]

GENERAL POWERS AND DUTIES OF LOCAL BOARDS

The powers of local boards have been judicially described in the following language:

> The school board has and can exercise those powers that are granted in express words; those fairly implied in or necessarily incidental to the powers expressly granted, and those essential to the declared objects and purposes of the corporation.[4]

While this definition of the authority of local boards of education is deeply rooted in the law and accepted by courts in all the states, not all courts agree in applications to specific cases. The legal definition of school board authority is essentially a narrow one, but great freedom is granted courts in determining whether a particular power can be classified as "fairly implied" or "necessarily incidental." In concrete situations courts of many states have gone exceedingly far in finding legal justifications for holding that a contested power of local boards was in fact implied when the aim of the local board was deemed clearly worth while educationally. The following chapters contain numerous examples of situations in which local boards, in the absence of express statutory authority, have performed acts of educational significance and have had their actions sustained by courts under broad interpretations of "implied powers." Frequently decisions have been reached after the courts have considered a multiplicity of factors which would have to be evaluated on other than strictly legal bases in circumstances where applicable legal precedents or doctrines were not available.

The history of public education is replete with developments which began with a local board's instituting an innovation carefully predetermined to effect desirable change in educational practice where statutes were silent on the matter. When such an innovation was challenged as being beyond the power of the board, the court was faced with the problem of deciding between upholding the innovation as an implied power or striking it down as an action beyond board powers. Public education has been substantially aided by the general disposition of courts to interpret implied powers broadly. It is necessary, of course, to point out that in many instances local school boards have not been judicially supported. Much of the remainder of this volume is devoted to objective analysis and synthesis of cases which illustrate and illuminate the seemingly simple but actually exceedingly complex situation posed by the general question: Does a local board of education have a specific implied power?

The distinction between actions where a board has abused its discretion and where it has exceeded its powers must be borne in mind. A particular act may be within the express or implied powers of a board and yet be subject to judicial bar if it can be shown that the board acted arbitrarily, capriciously, unreasonably, or in a discriminatory fashion. For example, it is universally true that a local board has the power to establish rules and regulations governing pupil conduct. Yet this undisputed power is subject to judicial interpretations as to whether the board abused its discretion in the exercise of the power in a given situation.

If a board is not already authorized to take certain action, it can acquire authority to perform the act only by statutory enactment. However, a board of education may not refuse to act on a matter where it legally has no discretionary power to decide how or whether to act. Such duties are called ministerial, as differentiated from discretionary. In such a situation the board can be compelled to act either by the state directly or through the courts upon application of one who has a direct interest in the action sought. In a recent case where a local board contended that it had no funds to comply with a state law related to retirement benefits for veterans the court said:

> Assuredly ... [a local school board] cannot annihilate an act of the Legislature by its failure or refusal to provide funds necessary for its mandatory obedience.[5]

While the distinction between ministerial and discretionary duties is often difficult to make, clear examples of the former would include providing courses in state-mandated subjects and following statutory procedures related to pupil transportation. Often a single duty has both ministerial and discretionary aspects. Awarding a contract to the lowest responsible bidder may be a ministerial duty, but discretion would be involved in determination of responsibility of a bidder.

CORPORATE NATURE OF SCHOOL BOARDS

The authority of a local board of education lies in the board as a corporate body. The board legally is the administrative body for the school district, and its power and duties are essentially those of the district. The board exists apart from the individuals composing it. Thus a change in board membership does not change the legal status of the board.

Members of boards of education as individuals cannot exercise the corporate powers of the board. The Supreme Court of Appeals of West Virginia described the legal status of an individual member as follows:

> ... a member of the board individually has no authority of any kind in connection with the schools of his county, except that the president, as such, is required to sign orders, contracts and so forth. The board of education can only act as a board, and when the board is not in session the members, severally or jointly, have no more authority to interfere with schools or school matters than any other citizen of the county.[6]

Actions to be legally binding must be taken by the board as a whole according to statutory and common law procedures. Legal aspects of school board procedure are discussed in Chapter IX. Likewise liabilities of school board members as individuals differ from those of the board as a legal entity. This point is elaborated upon in Chapter X.

The powers and duties of a board of education must be exercised by the board as a whole. Boards may not divest themselves of powers delegated to them by the legislature. They cannot give committees of the board, employees of the board, other governmental officials or private persons the authority to perform acts over which the board as a whole has discretionary power. Thus, if the power of employing teachers resides in the board, as it does in almost all jurisdictions, the board as a whole must take action if a teacher is to be legally employed. The basis of the non-delegability doctrine is rooted in public policy. The board is created to perform certain functions for the public. Unless they are performed by the board members as a body, the purpose of having a board is thwarted. This does not mean that individuals or committees of the board cannot be assigned such functions as fact-finding or drawing up recommendations for board action. Such an operational procedure would be desirable at times and would not be contrary to law. The board as a whole, however, must review any recommendations and in an official action accept them before they become effective.

In one case it was contended that the work of a committee of the board of education in regard to purchase of desks was such that approval of the recommendation by the whole board was only perfunctory. The Supreme Court of New Jersey discussed the issue as follows:

. . . where such corporate action is necessary, the fact that the negotiations have been conducted by a committee for that purpose will not invalidate the resolution awarding the contract, provided the result of such negotiation is first reported to the corporate body, and there discussed and considered before final action.[7]

RELATIONS WITH THE COURTS

Of fundamental importance in understanding the relation of the courts to the local school board is the principle that the courts will not interfere with a decision of a board of education in an area in which the board has power to act unless it can be shown that the board abused its discretion. In the language of one court:

> In the absence of fraud, abuse of discretion, arbitrariness or unreasonableness, . . . this court will not interfere with . . . [the] authority nor substitute its judgment for that of . . . [the] board upon matters delegated to it to decide in conducting the affairs of its schools.[8]

Reasonableness is quite different from wisdom. Whether a rule is wise or in the best interests of the school district is for the school board and not the courts to decide. The necessity of such a proposition is evident, for if a court could pass on the wisdom of legislative acts (and adoption of rules by boards is legislative in character), the balance of power among the branches of government in the United States would be destroyed and a domination by the judiciary would result. When a board of education acts in an unwise fashion, redress lies at the polls, not in the courtrooms.

What constitutes unreasonableness of a board regulation is a question of law to be determined by the court rather than a matter of fact for jury determination. A rule can be held unreasonable in terms either of its subject matter or of its enforcement. A presumption exists that a board rule is reasonable; the complaining party must prove unreasonableness.

One court, in a leading case, has stated the principle as follows:

> The question, therefore, is not whether we approve this rule as one we would have made as directors of the district, nor are we required to find whether it was essential to the maintenance of discipline. On the contrary, we must uphold the rule unless we find that the directors have clearly abused their discretion, and that the rule is not one reasonably calculated to effect the purpose intended, that is, of promoting discipline in the school. . . .[9]

CITATIONS

1. State *ex rel.* Clark v. Haworth, 122 Ind. 462, 23 N.E. 946 (1890).
2. Borough of Wilkinsburg v. School District of Wilkinsburg, 365 Pa. 254, 74 A.2d 138 (1950).
3. City of Louisville v. Commonwealth, 134 Ky. 488, 121 S.W. 411 (1909).
4. Board of Education of Oklahoma City v. Cloudman, 185 Okl. 400, 92 P.2d 837 (1939).
5. Race v. Board of Education, 37 N.J.Super. 333, 117 A.2d 312 (1955).
6. State *ex rel.* Rogers v. Board of Education of Lewis County, 125 W. Va. 579, 25 S.E.2d 537 (1943).
7. Kraft v. Board of Education, 67 N.J.L. 512, 51 A. 483 (1902).
8. Dworken v. Cleveland Board of Education, 108 N.E.2d 103 (Ohio 1951).
9. Pugsley v. Sellmeyer, 158 Ark. 247, 250 S.W. 538 (1923).

II

THE AUTHORITY OF SCHOOL BOARDS
IN RELATION TO PUPIL PERSONNEL

COMPULSORY ATTENDANCE

In General

State statutes regarding compulsory education of children in a certain age group are basic to the pattern of public education in the United States. These laws make it the duty of parents or guardians to see that their children are educated and provide penalties for noncompliance. Usually criteria for exemption, such as mental or physical disability or incorrigibility, are specified in the laws. Often in addition there are ages specified for eligibility to attend public schools. For example, in one state children of ages five to twenty may attend public schools until they complete a certain level whereas those of ages seven to sixteen are required to attend or obtain equivalent education elsewhere. While it might seem at first as if there could be little controversy regarding compulsory attendance laws, in reality there has been much litigation, and cases in this area continue to arise. Also it should be noted that in almost every state responsibility for enforcing these laws lies at the local level.

Uniformly the constitutionality of such laws has been upheld with the limitation that attendance may not be required at a public school. This proviso is exceedingly important, it being based on a decision of the United States Supreme Court in 1925 invalidating an Oregon law requiring children between the ages of eight and sixteen to attend public schools. That opinion indicated, however, that the state has the power "reasonably to regulate all schools, to inspect, supervise, and examine them, their teachers and pupils."[1]

Home Instruction

Whether compulsory education laws are satisfied by home instruction is a moot point. The cases are not in agreement. It goes without saying that if the home instruction is not deemed equivalent to that offered at a school it cannot be substituted. But what constitutes equivalent instruction? This is the heart of the numerous home instruction cases.

Some courts take the view that home instruction never can be equivalent. One in New Jersey has stated:

> I incline to the opinion that education is no longer concerned merely with the acquisition of facts; the instilling of worthy habits, attitudes, appreciations, and skills is far more important than mere imparting of subject matter. . . . Education must impart to the child the way to live. This brings me to the belief that, in a cosmopolitan area such as we live in, with all the complexities of life, . . . it is almost impossible for a child to be adequately taught at home.[2]

Another has said:

> The underlying philosophy of modern life is that people, through social intercourse with one another, shall live in amity, and absorb unto ourselves that which is good in our neighbor, and shun that which is bad. . . . The entire lack of free association with other children being denied [the children involved] . . . leads me to the conclusion that they are not receiving education equivalent to that provided in the public schools. . . .[3]

Other courts examine closely the quality of the instruction given at home before deciding on equivalency. As a New York court reasoned:

> The object of a compulsory education law is to see that children are not left in ignorance, that from some source they will receive instruction that will fit them for their place in society. Provided the instruction given is adequate and the sole purpose of nonattendance at school is not to evade the statute, instruction given to a child at home by its parent, who is competent to teach, should satisfy the requirements of the compulsory education law.

In this case a lower court judgment against the parent was reversed by the appellate court because the trial court had not admitted evidence regarding the proficiency of the children taught at home.[4]

Whether the parent or employed tutor involved in the home instruction has, or is eligible for, a teacher's credential for the grades taught is also an issue. In a recent California case it was held that such a credential was necessary under the law. The United States Supreme Court dismissed an appeal in this case "for want of a substantial federal question."[5] It is interesting to note that the same party was involved in the New York and California cases, the family having moved.

On the other hand in Illinois it was held that there was no violation of the law in a case of instruction at home by a mother who "had two years of college and some training in pedagogy and educational psychology," where there were regular hours of study, the proper subjects were taught, and the children were progressing satisfactorily.[6]

Religious Considerations

Religious grounds may be asserted as a basis for not complying with compulsory attendance laws. Parents may claim that their religious faith directs them to instruct their children at home. Uniformly the courts will not accept this as a valid exception *per se*. In the words of one court:

> Obviously, an illiterate parent cannot properly educate his child, nor can he, by attempting to do so, avoid his obligation to send it to school. No amount of religious fervor he may entertain in opposition to adequate instruction should be allowed to work a lifelong injury to his child. Nor should he, for this religious reason, be suffered to inflict another illiterate citizen on his community or his state.[7]

In a case decided in 1955, Buddhist parents offered as justification for failing to send a child to school the contention that Bible-reading and repeating the Lord's Prayer conflicted with his faith. In this instance the court did not look into whether or not home instruction was given, because it held that such instruction, to be considered in compliance with the compulsory attendance law, would have had to be approved by the superintendent or the board in advance of keeping the child home. This had not been done, and the parents were found guilty of violating the compulsory education law.[8]

Also convicted of violating a compulsory attendance law were Moslem parents who refused to send their child to school on Fridays (the sacred day of their religion). The opinion of the court in that case included this reasoning:

> The provision that children shall attend "continuously through the entire term" recognizes the obvious fact that each day's school work is built upon the lessons taught on the preceding day. It is virtually impossible prop-

erly to educate a child who is absent one day a week. Friday's instruction is the foundation for understanding Monday's lesson. By such regularly recurring absences the child loses not only one-fifth of the instruction, but the continuity of the course of study is broken and the pupil is not able to keep pace with his classmates.[9]

Other Issues

Not acceptable as a basis for nonattendance is the disagreement of a parent with a school regulation. A parent who objected to the school's running on daylight saving time (he believing in "God's time" and belonging to the Conference to Eliminate Daylight Saving) kept his children home a few days in protest and then sent them to school one hour late every day. Actually the school board had not officially adopted daylight saving time, as a statute required schools to observe standard time, but the board had adopted a resolution to have school open and close one hour earlier during the continuation of daylight saving time. The court found the parent guilty of violating the compulsory education law. Incidentally it did not find that the school board had violated the standard time statute.[10]

Likewise held subject to prosecution under the compulsory education statute was a parent who caused his daughter to be suspended by school authorities for disobedience at his command of a rule requiring children who did not bring food from home to eat in the school cafeteria.[11]

A justifiable reason for nonattendance is ill health. This exemption is implied if not explicit in the law. Occasionally, however, an alleged health reason may not be valid. In one case parents claimed a daughter's health was so poor that she should not attend. After three physicians examined the child and deemed her fit, a fourth issued a certificate to the effect that she should not attend school because of poor health. The evidence indicated that prior to trying to get an exemption from attendance the child had not been under a physician's care and that the only medication she received comprised patent medicines administered by the parents. The parents were found guilty when the court decided the child's health would not be endangered by attendance.[12]

If a child is handicapped, as distinguished from being in temporary poor health, special considerations arise. Here the statutes play a crucial role. Legislation pertaining to the handicapped, or exceptional children as they often are called, is being added at a rapid pace throughout the country. Some definitions are getting into laws and state department of education regulations. Also administrative machinery to identify the exceptional child is being developed. Legally, there are two distinct aspects of the problem: requiring those who can benefit from instruction to attend, and excluding those who cannot benefit or may interfere with the progress of normal children. One case involving both considerations arose when a school board assigned a child who had suffered infantile paralysis to a special ungraded school where work was on an individual basis dependent on the proficiency of the child. The parents refused to send the child to this school, and the board refused to permit the child to attend the regular graded school. In the subsequent prosecution under the attendance law, the school board was upheld, the court saying:

> The assigning of defendant's child to the Franklin [ungraded] School does not appear to be amenable to attack on the ground that it was an unreasonable exercise of authority. There was evident inability on the part of the child to meet the standards of the graded schools. It is in the record that he was an unfortunate victim of infantile paralysis, and that he suffers continually from pain. True, the child is sensitive and it was the fear of defendant that, being compelled to attend the Franklin School, the child might become embittered against attending any school on account of the fact that children in the graded schools were inclined to refer to the Franklin School as the "dumb school" and to treat discourteously the pupils there attending. . . . From the entire record, there does not appear unreasonableness such as would warrant holding that the board exceeded the authority intended to be granted to school boards to determine where pupils may attend school.[13]

Also judicially upheld has been the exclusion from regular school of a child on the grounds that, although the pupil was mentally normal, his physical condition produced a "nauseating and depressing" effect on the teachers and class.[14] Courts also consider the positive benefits to a handicapped child obtained from going to a special school having facilities to compensate for his infirmity. In one case a court, over the protest of the parents, upheld the committal of a totally deaf child to a distant state insituation for the deaf rather than permitting him to attend the rural school near his home.[15]

In an increasing number of jurisdictions the responsibility of the local board does not end with the exclusion of an exceptional child. Often it must send the child to a neighboring district where facilities are available.

Payment of expenses for tuition and transportation in such cases is normally determined by the statutes.

A word should be said about the relationship of married pupils to compulsory attendance laws. Normally, a married pupil is not subject to these laws. On the other hand, marriage *per se* is not justifiable grounds for excluding a pupil.

ADMISSION POLICIES

In General

Attendance at the public schools of a given state is subject to constitutional and legislative control. Any right to attend must be found in the legal structure of the state. Some states have gone further than others in outlining regulations relative to prerequisites for attendance. Regardless, local school boards have implied powers to set up reasonable rules for admission to supplement state-level policies and not inconsistent with them.

Vaccination

Probably the most litigated admission policy is that pertaining to vaccination. Although the largest numbers of the cases arose in days when inoculations were less generally accepted as effective protections against disease, such cases still occur in modern times. That a state law empowering local authorities to require everyone to be vaccinated is not in violation of the United States Constitution was decided back in 1905, when the United States Supreme Court upheld a Massachusetts law to this effect in the words:

> But the liberty secured by the Constitution . . . does not import an absolute right in each person to be, at all times and in all circumstances, wholly free from restraint. There are manifold restraints to which every person is necessarily subject for the common good. On any other basis organized society could not exist with safety to its members. . . . Real liberty for all could not exist under the operation of a principle which recognizes the right of each individual person to use his own, whether in respect of his person or his property, regardless of the injury that may be done to others. This Court has more than once recognized it as a fundamental principle that "persons and property are subjected to all kinds of restraints and burdens in order to secure the general comfort, health, and prosperity of the state. . . ."[16]

In 1922 the United States Supreme Court upheld the constitutionality of a law specifically making vaccination a prerequisite to school attendance.[17]

It should be emphasized that these decisions leave the matter within the jurisdiction of the individual states, there being no federal question. Courts in the various states have handled the matter in different ways, depending to a large extent on the wording of applicable statutes. No state court has invalidated a statute which required or authorized local authorities to require vaccination before entrance to school. Difficulties arise when there is no statute and the local board institutes a vaccination requirement of its own. The cases are not in agreement in this situation unless an epidemic is reasonably imminent, in which circumstance local boards generally have been held to have such implied power. Thus, in the absence of a controlling statute, court precedents in a given state must be checked to obtain the correct rule.

Age

Age requirements for admission also create problems. If the law specifies that children either are entitled to, or required to, attend school at a given age, does that mean immediately after the child's birthday? The only common sense answer to this would seem to have to be "no." It becomes necessary, therefore, for boards of education to set up "cut-off" dates for birthdays of children to be admitted in a given semester or year. The courts recognize that some such rules are necessary for the orderly conduct of the school. One pertinent case involved a rule that children under seven years of age could not attend school unless they entered at the beginning of the fall term or within four weeks thereafter or unless they were qualified to enter classes existing at the time they entered. In holding the regulation to be reasonable the court said:

> Grading is a permitted, if not an essential, feature of the school system. The introduction to the school of a very young scholar, late in the school year, if the scholar is not qualified to enter existing classes, would tend strongly to impair the efficiency of the school, and so prevent the other scholars from obtaining from it such . . . training as would enable them to proceed with their education in due course. [17a]

A contrary view was expressed by another court, however, where a board had denied entrance to a pupil who became of age thirty-one days after the beginning of the term under a rule providing that proper age had to be reached during the first month of the term. While not denying the board's authority to set up reasonable age requirements, it felt this one was not reasonable.[18]

It is interesting to note that both of these cases were decided around 1900. Since then there has been no case in an appellate state court precisely on this point. It seems clear, however, that increased enrollment makes the need to establish cut-off dates imperative, and except in an unusual fact situation, it is doubtful that today a court would interfere with a local board's action in this area.

In a 1953 Colorado case it was held that a cut-off date specified in a board rule as applicable "to all regular residents of the district" would not apply to transfer students. The child in question had attended school in another state in the fall and sought admission to the first grade in January. The court was persuaded by the fact that the child had actually attended school "for as many months as the children of the first grade class to which he sought admission" despite the fact that evidence showed the parents had tried unsuccessfully to get him admitted in the fall, then had sent him to enroll in the schools of another state, and now claimed that he should be admitted as a transfer student. The court made a strict interpretation of the wording of the board rule.[19]

Residence

Many problems arise in connection with policies related to residence of pupils for school purposes. Generally this is controlled by statute, and in order for a child to have the privilege of attending free the schools of a district, he must be a resident of the district. Just what constitutes residence is not always clear. The majority rule is that residence for school purposes does not mean that the child has to have his legal domicile there. (Domicile includes the intention to remain in the location indefinitely. One may have several residences but only one domicile.) If a child is actually living in a district, he is generally entitled to enter the school there, unless entrance in the school was the purpose of his living there.[20] Thus, a child boarding out in a district for reasons other than school attendance would be entitled to go to the school in that district regardless of where his father lived. In a situation where a child's father owns a business in one district and lives in another, normally the child would be entitled to free schooling only in the district where he lives, notwithstanding the fact that his father pays taxes in the other district.[21]

Fees

What, if any, fees may be charged pupils in the public schools has not been clearly determined by court rulings. The answer depends basically on the wording of the state constitution regarding the public school system and further on the applicable statutes of the state. Generally, tuition, registration, or matriculation fees cannot be charged resident pupils if the state constitution or statutes provide for free public education.[22] This has been held even if a pupil through his own lack of application stays more than four years in high school. He is entitled to attend free if he is within the age limit for which attendance at the public schools is permitted.[23] Nonresident pupils, however, are usually subject to a tuition fee imposed by the receiving board. The tuition fee may be paid by the district where the child resides or by his parent. If the district of residence does not provide a required grade or course, the district must pay the tuition fee of the pupil in the receiving district. If the grade or course is not mandated by the state, generally the option of paying or not paying tuition for a student living in the district but going to school in another district lies in the discretion of the board, in the absence of a statute covering the point.

Admission to a Particular Grade or School

School boards have the right to set up reasonable scholarship requirements for admission to a particular grade or class. This is true both for students already in the school system and for students transferring from other districts or from private schools. Courts will not interfere unless arbitrary, unreasonable, or capricious action can be shown. One court stated:

> The care and management of schools which is vested in the school committee includes the establishment and maintenance of standards for the promotion of pupils from one grade to another and for their continuance as members of any particular class. So long as the school committee act in good faith their conduct in formulating and applying standards and making decisions touching this matter is not subject to review by any other tribunal. It is obvious that efficiency of instruction depends in no small degree upon this feature of our school system. It is an educational question, the final determination of which is vested by law in the public officers charged with the performance of that important duty.[24]

Recently a New York court upheld a school board's determination that a child be placed in kindergarten rather than first grade over the protest of a parent who argued that maintenance of kindergartens was optional and that a five-year-old under state law had a right to attend public school. The court held that once a kindergarten is established, even though establishment is optional, it becomes a part of the school system, and while the child had a right to attend school, the grade assignment was in the discretion of the school board. The court further ruled that the child had to be admitted to school on a basis of age, but once admitted, "the board of education has the power to provide rules and regulations for promotion from grade to grade, based not on age, but on training, knowledge, and ability."[25]

Both old and recent cases clearly point out that place of attendance is up to the board. A pupil is not entitled as a matter of right to attend the school closest to his home, or any other particular school.[26] Such determinations are in the power of the school board, and can be set aside by courts only if they are unreasonable or arbitrarily applied.

In 1954 the United States Supreme Court banned the use of race as the sole criterion for admission or assignment to any public school. The unanimous decision was based on a finding that compulsory racial segregation was in violation of the Fourteenth Amendment because "separate educational facilities are inherently unequal."[27]

RULES OF CONDUCT

In General

School boards have the authority, implied if not express, to adopt reasonable rules and regulations for the operation of the schools not in conflict with constitutional or statutory provisions. The key point is the word "reasonable." Whether a rule is reasonable is a question of law for the courts, and they have heard hundreds of cases involving the interpretation of that word. A rule is not reasonable in the abstract, but can be reasonable only in a context of application. Obviously circumstances condition reasonableness. Thus, particular fact situations are decisive in the determination of whether a regulation may legally be enforced. This section will treat the validity of rules; modes of enforcement will be dealt with in the next section.

There is generally a legal presumption of validity of a board rule, which presumption must be refuted by the complaining party. Also, as discussed in Chapter I, the courts will not substitute their judgment as to the wisdom of a rule for that of the local board of education, the legally constituted body to operate the schools. The situation has been described by one court as follows:

> . . . the unreasonableness of . . . a rule is a judicial question and the courts have the right of review. They will not hesitate to intervene in proper cases. In doing so, however, it will be kept in mind that the local board is the final authority so long as it acts in good faith and refrains from adopting regulations which are clearly arbitrary or unreasonable. It will be remembered also that respect for constituted authority and obedience thereto is an essential lesson to qualify one for the duties of citizenship and that the school is an appropriate place to teach that lesson.[28]

Furthermore, the right of administrators and teachers to adopt reasonable rules not in conflict with laws and regulations of higher legal authorities is clear.

Rules related broadly to conduct of pupils may be classified as those governing conduct on school premises and those governing conduct off the premises. In either situation, the following guide set out long ago by a Wisconsin court applies:

> Any rule or regulation which has for its object anything outside of the instruction of the pupil—the order requisite for instruction—is beyond the province of the board of education to adopt.[29]

Rules Applying to Conduct on School Grounds

It would seem that cases involving the clothes and appearance of pupils would be numerous, but such is not the situation. Certainly there are many threats of legal action and undoubtedly some trial court cases which have not been appealed and therefore are not recorded. Or maybe common sense on the parts of both parents and school authorities has generally prevailed. The few cases in appellate courts, however, give some guides.

The following board rule was challenged in 1923 in Arkansas:

> The wearing of transparent hosiery, low-necked dresses, or any style of clothing tending toward immodesty in dress, or the use of face paint or cosmetics, is prohibited.

The court refused to invalidate the rule in an opinion which included these words:

> We are unwilling to say, as a matter of law, that a local condition might not exist which would make a rule of this character desirable in aid of the discipline of the school, and we therefore decline to annul it, for we will not annul a rule of the kind unless a valid reason for doing so is made to appear; whereas, to uphold it, we are not required to find a valid reason for its promulgation.[30]

Very similar reasoning was used by another court to uphold a prohibition against wearing metal heel-plates.[31] On the other hand, a rule mandating the wearing of cap and gown for commencement exercises was held void when it was used as a basis for withholding a girl's diploma, although refusal to allow her to participate in public ceremonies without cap and gown would be legally permissible according to the Supreme Court of Iowa. The court stated:

> The wearing of a cap and gown on commencement night has no relation to educational values, the discipline of the school, scholastic grades, or intellectual advancement. Such a rule may be justified in some instances from the viewpoint of economy, but from a legal viewpoint, the board might as well attempt to direct the wearing of overalls by the boys and calico dresses by the girls.[32]

Regulations pertaining to loss or damage of property by pupils are not enforceable, according to the few cases on the point, if the destruction is due to negligence and not intention on the part of the student. The basis of this position is, in the words of one court:

> The State does not deprive its citizens of their property or their liberty, or of any rights, except as a punishment for a crime. It would be very harsh and obviously unjust to deprive a child of education for the reason that through accident and without intention of wrong he destroyed property of the school district. Doubtless a child can be expelled from school as a punishment for breach of discipline or for offenses against good morals, but not for innocent acts.[33]

However, it has been held that pupils whose parents are financially able may be required to pay a deposit which can be forfeited if free textbooks are not properly handled.[34]

Rules prohibiting the leaving of the school premises during the school day, except for children going home to lunch with written requests from parents, have been sustained. This was true even in a case where a father wanted his children to eat the midday meal regularly with him at a downtown hotel. The court upheld the rule in the absence of a showing that the children's health was endangered by the rule. But the court cautioned that elasticity in enforcement was needed.[35]

A 1955 Kentucky decision upheld as reasonable the following rule:

> No one, while in school, shall be allowed to enter the restaurant of Mr. Russell or any other business establishment in the town without permission from 8:15 A.M. until 3:00 P.M.

Russell's restaurant adjoined the school, and it was not denied that the rule was designed to encourage children to purchase lunches in the school cafeteria. The appellate court reversed the judgment of the trial court and held the rule valid in the following language:

> It is common knowledge that children, if allowed to depend upon their selection, often indulge themselves in unbalanced diets. Furthermore, if uncontrolled at table young children are apt to engage in rough or uncouth practices and conduct. If the school lunch is to be successful, then all children who purchase their noon meal may be required to do so from the school lunchroom. The regulation appears to be for the common good of all children attending this school. . . .[36]

It should be noted, however, that board rules must not be designed to ruin someone's business. If ulterior motives of the board can be proved, the rule will not be judicially approved.

A matter that has been widely litigated is that of regulation of fraternities and sororities. Many states have statutes prohibiting the operation of secret societies in public schools. All that have been challenged have been held constitutional, the United States Supreme Court in 1915 having upheld one applying to state university students.[37] Generally, too, courts have upheld the right of local school authorities, regardless of permissive or mandatory statutes, to regulate secret societies operating within the schools provided it can be shown that such control is necessary to the discipline and well-being of the schools. The most common type of locally adopted regulation denies to members of secret societies certain privileges enjoyed by other students, such as participation in "extracurricular" activities. Several recent decisions have affirmed that restrictions on fraternities and sororities are within the power of school authorities and do not in general infringe the individual rights of parents or students.[38]

Rules Applying to Conduct off School Grounds

The authority of the school board over conduct of school pupils is not limited to acts occurring on school premises. As one court put it in an early case:

> The view that acts, to be within the authority of the school board and teachers for discipline and correction, must be done within school hours, is narrow, and without regard to the spirit of the law and the best interest of our common schools. It is in conflict, too, with [legal] authority.[39]

Furthermore, in the language of another court:

> Examination of the authorities clearly reveals the true test of the teacher's right and jurisdiction to punish for offenses not committed on the school property or going and returning therefrom, but after the return of the pupil to the parental abode, to be not the time or place of the offense, but its effect upon the morale and efficiency of the school, whether it in fact is detrimental to its good order, and to the welfare and advancement of the pupils therein.[40]

Thus, school boards are empowered to adopt reasonable rules covering any conduct which could be proved to a court to be detrimental to the good order and proper operation of the schools. Rules, for example, that pupils go directly home from school and that they refrain from fighting or using profane language while on the way home from school have been held enforceable. Also, it is pertinent to note that the fact that activities of secret societies are held off of school premises does not necessarily prevent the enforcement of a rule prohibiting membership during a school semester.[41] Also judicially validated was a rule that there should be no playing of football either on the school grounds or under the auspices of the school off the grounds. The case in point arose when a team of students advertised themselves as the high school team and played a game at a fair ground. The resultant suspension of the pupils was sustained by a court.[42]

There is some conflict in the few old cases related to prohibitions against students attending social functions on nights before school sessions.[43] So is there in relation to specificity of rules related to homework. For example, a rule requiring pupils to stay at home and study from 7:00 to 9:00 P.M. has been held unreasonable,[44] whereas one requiring the working of some arithmetic problems at home has been upheld as being within the power of school authorities.[45]

Control in Absence of Regulations

Obviously school boards, administrators, and teachers cannot antici-
pate every act which will interfere with the conduct of the schools and set
up a rule to deal with it. This statement applies to conduct off, as well as
on, school grounds. In a much quoted old case a teacher was upheld in
the corporal punishment of a student the morning following the student's
having shown disrespect for him an hour and a half after school the day
before by calling him "Old Jack Seaver" in the presence of fellow pupils.[46]

Furthermore, the punishable action does not have to be in the presence of the teacher. This was held in a case where some pupils had published in a newspaper a poem ridiculing the rules of the school.[47] Also,
the offense may have taken place after the child reached home. Indeed,
in one case, a boy was on his mother's property when he annoyed and
abused small girls on their way home from school; yet the court held such
conduct punishable.[48]

The judicial attitude in regard to punishment when no specific rule
has been broken is well summed up in an old leading case as follows:

> One of the most thoroughly established rules in the government of a
> school permits a teacher to punish a pupil for a violation of good order
> and necessary discipline, and the reasonableness of such a rule, as an ab-
> stract proposition, has never, as we are aware, been seriously ques-
> tioned. . . .[49]

ENFORCEMENT OF RULES (PUNISHMENTS)

In General

It is clear that a reasonable rule might be unreasonably enforced; that
is, the punishment might be too grave to be warranted by the offense, it
might infringe a right of the child or his parent, it might interfere with
the child's health, or it might have some result which would render it unacceptable to a court as a means of promoting the best interests of the
school and the pupil. In the cases discussed in the preceding sections
courts often pointed out that they were assuming reasonable enforcement
of the rules they were sustaining. "In the enforcement of every law there
should be brought into play the element of common sense."[50]

Detention after school for a reasonable period has been sustained.
Likewise, withholding of privileges as a punishment is recognized. Care

should be taken to be sure that what is withheld, however, is a privilege, not a right of a student. Academic punishments for misbehavior are not in general looked on any more favorably by courts than by most educators. Withholding of diplomas, for example, as a disciplinary measure has been judicially disapproved.[51] In one case it was upheld, apparently because the student was forewarned and knew the penalty for the act he deliberately performed—joining a fraternity, which was forbidden by a statute specifying the penalty of no diploma.[52]

Suspension and Expulsion

Suspension and expulsion are judicially recognized methods of preserving discipline in the schools, suspension connoting a temporary banishment usually until something is done or some circumstances alleviated, and expulsion being of a more permanent nature. Many states have statutes pertaining to suspension and expulsion. Frequently these list causes for exclusion, and several indicate procedures to be followed, particularly for expulsion. In many states only the local board of education in a corporate action has the power of expulsion, and in some states a pupil must be afforded a hearing before expulsion. Since this is a grave penalty it must be exercised with care. If the proper procedure is followed, however, so long as the rule broken is within the power of the board to make and is reasonable, or the conduct of the pupil is patently such that his continued presence in the school would be deleterious to the welfare of the other pupils, courts generally have sustained the legality of suspension or expulsion as a disciplinary measure.

If a pupil is wrongfully expelled, he and his parent are not without legal redress. Liabilities of board members in connection with wrongful suspension or expulsion are discussed in Chapter X.

Corporal Punishment

The legality of corporal punishment as a method for enforcing discipline has been tested in the courts since public schools were established and there is no sign of an abatement of the cases. Actually the "rule" is rather easy to state but is hard to apply in given fact situations. In one of the leading cases it is put this way:

> ... the teacher is, within reasonable bounds, the substitute for the parent, exercising his delegated authority. He is vested with the power to ad-

minister moderate correction, with the proper instrument, . . . which ought to have some reference to the character of the offense, the sex, age, size, and physical strength of the pupil. When the teacher keeps within the circumscribed sphere of his authority, the degree of correction must be left to his discretion, as it is to the parent, under like circumstances. Within this limit, he has the authority to determine the gravity . . . of the offense, and to mete out to the offender the punishment which he thinks his conduct justly merits. . . . All of the authorities agree that he will not be permitted to deal brutally with his victim so as to endanger life, limb or health. . . .[53]

The concept of the teacher standing in place of the parent *(in loco parentis)* is well established and is essentially the key to the standard of reasonableness in regard to punishment. Might a responsible parent under similar circumstances have inflicted such corporal punishment? This is the common law standard and is applicable both in civil and criminal proceedings which may be brought against a teacher who has corporally punished a pupil. Only a few states through statute or regulation of the state board of education bar corporal punishment or circumscribe its application. Clearly, a local board may adopt a regulation on the matter, and many throughout the country have done so. On the other hand, some states have made explicit in statute the common law authority of the teacher to administer corporal punishment. Depending on the wording of the law, local boards might or might not be able to reduce the teacher's authority in their districts.

Legal actions in this area generally are brought against the school personnel inflicting the punishment. In one old case, however, a board member forcibly ejected a pupil from a school after the pupil used profane language when the board member asked him if he could not do a better job of removing chalkmarks he had put on a school stovepipe. The court, taking into account his position, held the board member not liable for assault and battery.[54]

The privilege of school personnel to punish corporally has been recently restated by the Supreme Court of Alabama as follows:

A schoolmaster is regarded as standing in *loco parentis* and has the authority to administer moderate correction to pupils under his care. To be guilty of an assault and battery, the teacher must not only inflict on the child immoderate chastisement, but he must do so with legal malice or wicked motives or he must inflict some permanent injury. In determining the reasonableness of the punishment or the extent of malice, proper matters for consideration are the instrument used and the nature of the offense committed by the child, the age and physical condition of the child, and the other attendant circumstances.[55]

Another recent opinion by an Ohio court on the point added the following:

> . . . there is a presumption of correctness of the teacher's actions. . . . there is a presumption that the teacher acts in good faith.[56]

CITATIONS

1. Pierce v. Society of Sisters, 268 U.S. 510, 45 S.Ct. 571 (1925).
2. Stephens v. Bongart, 15 N.J. Misc. 80, 189 A. 131 (1937).
3. Knox v. O'Brien, 7 N.J.Super. 608, 72 A.2d 389 (1950).
4. People v. Turner, 277 App. Div. 317, 98 N.Y.S.2d 886 (1950).
5. People v. Turner, 121 Cal. App.2d 861, 263 P.2d 685 (1953). App. dism. 347 U.S. 972, 74 S.Ct. 785 (1954).
6. People v. Levinsen, 404 Ill. 574, 90 N.E.2d 213 (1950).
7. Rice v. Commonwealth, 188 Va. 224, 49 S.E.2d 342 (1948).
8. Commonwealth v. Renfrew, 126 N.E.2d 109 (Mass. 1955).
9. Commonwealth v. Bey, 166 Pa. Super. 136, 70 A.2d 693 (1950).
10. Commonwealth v. Schrock, 77 D. & C. 258 (Pa. 1952).
11. Bishop v. Houston Independent School District, 119 Tex. 403, 29 S.W.2d 312 (1930).
12. Parr v. State, 117 Ohio St. 23, 157 N.E. 555 (1927).
13. State v. Ghrist, 222 Ia. 1069, 270 N.W. 376 (1936).
14. State *ex rel.* Beattie v. Board of Education of Antigo, 169 Wis. 231, 172 N.W. 153 (1919).
15. State Board of Education v. Petty, 241 Ia. 506, 41 N.W.2d 672 (1950).
16. Jacobson v. Commonwealth of Massachusetts, 197 U.S. 11, 25 S.Ct. 358 (1905).
17. Zucht v. King, 260 U.S. 174, 43 S.Ct. 24 (1922).
17a. Alvord v. Inhabitants of Town of Chester, 180 Mass. 20, 61 N.E. 263 (1901).
18. Moline Board of Education v. Bolton, 85 Ill. App. 92 (1899).
19. Simonson v. School District No. 14, 127 Colo. 575, 258 P.2d 1128 (1953).
20. Cline v. Knight, 111 Colo. 8, 137 P.2d 680 (1943).
21. Cape Girardeau School District v. Frye, 225 S.W.2d 484 (Mo. 1949).

22. Dowell v. School District No. 1, 220 Ark. 828, 250 S.W.2d 127 (1952).
23. Batty v. Board of Education of Williston, 67 N.D. 6, 269 N.W. 49 (1936).
24. Barnard v. Shelburne, 216 Mass. 19, 102 N.E. 1095 (1913).
25. Isquith v. Levitt, 285 App. Div. 833, 137 N.Y.S.2d 497 (1955).
26. Howell School Board District v. Hubbartt, 246 Ia. 1265, 70 N.W.2d 531 (1955).
27. Brown v. Board of Education, 347 U.S. 483, 74 S.Ct. 686 (1954).
28. Coggins v. Board of Education of Durham, 223 N.C. 763, 28 S.E.2d 527 (1944).
29. State v. Fond du Lac Board of Education, 63 Wis. 234, 23 N.W. 102 (1885).
30. Pugsley v. Sellmeyer, 158 Ark. 247, 250 S.W. 538 (1923).
31. Stromberg v. French, 60 N.D. 750, 236 N.W. 477 (1931).
32. Valentine v. Independent School District, 191 Ia. 1100, 183 N.W. 434 (1921).
33. Perkins v. Independent School District, 56 Ia. 476, 9 N.W. 356 (1880).
34. Segar v. Rockford Board of Education, 317 Ill. 418, 148 N.E. 289 (1925).
35. Flory v. Smith, 145 Va. 164, 134 S.E. 360 (1926).
36. Casey County Board of Education v. Luster, 282 S.W.2d 333 (Ky. 1955).
37. Waugh v. University of Mississippi, 237 U.S. 589, 35 S.Ct. 720 (1915).
38. Burkitt v. School District No. 1, 195 Ore. 471, 246 P.2d 566 (1952).
39. Burdick v. Babcock, 31 Ia. 562 (1871).
40. O'Rourke v. Walker, 102 Conn. 130, 128 A. 25 (1925).
41. Wilson v. Abilene Independent School District, 190 S.W.2d 406 (Tex. Civ. App. 1945).
42. Kinzer v. Independent School District, 129 Ia. 441, 105 N.W. 686 (1906).
43. Cf. Mangum v. Keith, 147 Ga. 603, 95 S.E. 1 (1918), and Dritt v. Snodgrass, 66 Mo. 286 (1877).
44. Hobbs v. Germany, 94 Miss. 469, 49 So. 515 (1909).
45. Bolding v. State, 23 Tex. App. 172, 4 S.W. 579 (1887).
46. Lander v. Seaver, 32 Vt. 114 (1859).
47. State ex rel. Dresser v. District Board, 135 Wis. 619, 116 N.W. 232 (1908).
48. O'Rourke v. Walker, supra note 40.
49. Fertich v. Michener, 111 Ind. 47, 11 N.E. 605, Reh. 14 N.E. 68 (1887).

50. Flory v. Smith, *supra* note 35.
51. Valentine v. Independent School District, *supra* note 32.
52. Steele v. Sexton, 253 Mich. 32, 234 N.W. 436 (1931).
53. Boyd v. State, 88 Ala. 169, 7 So. 268 (1890)
54. Peck v. Smith, 41 Conn. 442 (1874).
55. Suits v. Glover, 260 Ala. 449, 71 So.2d 49 (1954).
56. State v. Lutz, 113 N.E.2d 757 (Ohio 1953).

III

THE AUTHORITY OF SCHOOL BOARDS
IN RELATION TO CURRICULUM

IN GENERAL

What goes on in the schools of a district is the heart of the responsibility of the local board of education. The word "curriculum" is used in this chapter in a broad sense to encompass all the learning experiences a pupil may encounter under the sponsorship of the schools. Some activities will be compulsory so far as the student is concerned, and others will be optional; but if they are made available on either basis, they are part of the curriculum provided for by the local school board.

In carrying out its responsibility for the curriculum, the local board of education is obliged to operate within the framework of state-level constitutional prescriptions, statutes, and regulations. Also it must be careful not to infringe rights guaranteed by the United States Constitution to taxpayers, parents, or pupils.

STATE–LOCAL RELATIONS

The states vary widely in regard to number and specificity of prescriptions related to the curriculum of the public schools. Also they differ in regard to source of prescriptions (that is, state constitution, state statute, state board of education regulation, or rule of the chief state school officer). Every state, however, in some legal way or other, requires that certain things be taught in the public schools and that other things not be taught. Beyond these positive and negative prescriptions local boards have exceedingly broad discretionary powers. It should be noted, however, that often school codes are not clear on a point in controversy and judicial decisions are needed to settle the issue. Hence, an understanding of curricular powers of local boards must ultimately be based on an analysis and synthesis of pertinent court opinions.

It is well established that the state, through the legislature, can require that certain subjects be taught. In such circumstances, the local board is bound to provide for these subjects. Furthermore, when a subject is required by the state, financial resources to support it properly must be made available locally. According to several courts, if the local board must operate a certain program it must be empowered to finance the program. A contrary construction would render state prescriptions meaningless. This line of judicial reasoning led a New York court to the conclusion that if a school district is required by the state to maintain night schools, it cannot fail to do so for alleged financial reasons. In the case in point, the court expressed sympathy with "the difficult problem that confronted the Board when it was suddenly called on to curtail useful school services to meet the cut in its appropriation" made by the municipal body on which it was fiscally dependent, but would not permit the termination of the offering.[1]

The highest court of Massachusetts has held that a statute requiring instruction to be given in the high school in such subjects as the local school board "considers expedient," is "equally compelling with the mandate requiring the maintenance of that school." Under this decision the city was required to provide financial support for the teaching of the subjects the school board "considered expedient" for the high school.[2]

When a statute stipulates that upon the petition of a certain number of parents of children attending school a subject should be introduced by local authorities, the local board has the duty to add the subject upon presentation of a petition. In an old Indiana case, while the board was required by the court to introduce the study of the German language upon a properly presented petition, it was deemed within the scope of the board to determine "the manner in which it is taught, and the extent to which it shall be studied."[3]

Also, as might be expected, when a new statutory mandate is forthcoming, reasonable time will be allowed by courts to local boards so that they may make administrative arrangements, such as getting funds, securing personnel, obtaining equipment. One court has said that "reasonable time to arrange matters" begins when the board is made aware of its new responsibility.[4]

Many states have mandatory statutes pertaining to the curriculum which may possibly be construed in more than one way. The general rule of statutory construction followed by courts is to give the statute the construction reasonably consistent with its purposes as determined by the court. A Michigan case is illustrative. The Michigan school code provided that:

> Instruction shall be given in physiology and hygiene, with a special reference to the nature of alcohol and narcotics, and their effect upon the human system. Such instruction shall be given by the aid of textbooks in the case of pupils who are able to read, and as thoroughly as in other studies pursued in the same school.

A teacher who had not yet taught hygiene and physiology in the sixth grade as of January 15 was discharged on this date for that reason. She claimed she intended to do so later in the year. She was following a course of study promulgated by the state superintendent of public instruction for use in one-room rural schools, in one of which she was teaching, and the syllabus did not provide for teaching hygiene and physiology. The trial court rejected the course of study argument as constituting no excuse and ruled that the law had been violated. The Supreme Court of Michigan, in reversing the judgment, stated that the requirement:

> . . . carries its own modicum of common sense, and all that need be done is to so read it. We find no conflict between the provisions of the statute and the "syllabus". Plaintiff's [the teacher's] contract was to teach a primary school. The superintendent of public instruction was required by statute to prepare the course of studies and did so. Plaintiff followed the course so prescribed, and it cannot be held that, in doing so, she breached the contract as a matter of law.[5]

Where a statute puts responsibility for prescribing a course of study in the hands of the state board of education, all local boards are bound to follow the program adopted by the state board. They cannot, in the words of one court:

> . . . adopt a course of study according to their own notions of what such a course should be; and if they were permitted to do so the result would be, in a large measure, to destroy that uniformity of our public

school system which is contemplated by the Constitution and laws of this state [Washington]. It is the duty of school directors, enjoined on them by law, to enforce the course of study prescribed by the State Board of Education, and not to adopt and enforce some other course, inconsistent therewith, which they may deem superior thereto.[6]

Just as a state may require certain curricular items to be taught, so may it prohibit certain teachings. Things proscribed by states include specific elements like the theory of evolution, vivisection, and communism, as well as broad areas such as sectarian doctrines and subversive doctrines. Local boards are bound to prevent such teachings as defined not only by the legislature but also by court interpretations. For example, in a few states courts have declared Bible-reading without comment as part of the opening exercises in schools to be in violation of general state constitutional prescriptions related to sectarian influences. A course in Bible study was banned by a Washington court as being in violation of constitutional provisions in that state against using public money for religious instruction or exercises. In this case the course was not required of students, but those who elected to take it were given academic credit for it. Although study was done outside the school, the school furnished an outline and gave an examination as a basis for the credit.[7]

It should be noted that there are limitations on what a state can prevent being taught. A United States Supreme Court decision invalidated a statutory prohibition against teaching a foreign language in grades lower than the ninth. The case arose in Nebraska after World War I. A teacher in a private school was convicted of teaching German as a distinct subject to children who had not passed the eighth grade. The statute was upheld as constitutional by the highest state court. It had been argued that "the purpose of the legislation was to promote civic development by inhibiting training and education of the immature in foreign tongues and ideals before they could learn English and acquire American ideals." The United States Supreme Court, however, struck down the statute. It found that the limitations on the rights of modern language teachers "to teach," of pupils "to acquire knowledge," and of parents "to control the education of their own," were not justifiable since there was no showing of harm which the state would have a right to prevent. In the words of the court:

No emergency has arisen which renders knowledge by a child of some language other than English so clearly harmful as to justify its inhibition with the consequent infringement of rights long freely enjoyed. We are constrained to conclude that the statute as applied is arbitrary and without reasonable relation to any end within the competency of the State.[8]

In addition to ordering local boards to do or not to do certain things related to the curriculum, state legislatures have enacted varying amounts of permissive legislation. This comprises statutes which specifically empower local boards to take certain actions, such as establish kindergartens or prescribe subjects to be taught on certain levels. Obviously under such laws the power of a local board to do something permitted by the statute is unchallengeable except on grounds that the enactment is unconstitutional.

ADDING COURSES AND PROGRAMS

No court has taken the position that local boards have no initiative in the area of curriculum. Indeed, a generalization to the effect that local boards have a vast amount of discretion to supplement state-level required courses and activities seems warranted by an analysis of the scores of pertinent decisions in high state courts. This discretion applies generally not only to addition of specific curricular elements, but also to determination of methods of carrying out both specific and general mandates.

Many of the state constitutions and the early statutes provided in varying phraseology that the legislatures should provide for a uniform and efficient system of education in the common branches throughout the state. As the need and the desire of citizens for more than elementary training of their children grew, local boards began adding what would now be called high school courses. This practice apparently spread rapidly with relatively little challenge from taxpayers. The legal landmark in this area is the famous Kalamazoo case of 1874. The question put squarely to the Supreme Court of Michigan was, Does a local board of education, in the absence of express legislative authority, have the power to maintain a high school? The reasoning behind the affirmative answer is summed up in the words of the court as follows:

We content ourselves with the statement that neither in our state policy, in our constitution, or in our laws, do we find the primary school districts restricted in the branches of knowledge which their officers may cause to be taught, or the grade of instruction that may be given, if their voters consent in regular form to bear the expense and raise the taxes for the purpose.[9]

Similarly reasoned judicial decisions have upheld local boards in establishing kindergartens. The courts are not in agreement, however, on the question of whether junior colleges may be established without express legislation.[10] A local board, it has been held, may establish an ungraded school and provide there for pupils who are unable for physical or mental reasons to progress in regular graded schools.[11]

There are many cases involving the power of local boards to offer courses of instruction not specifically set out in the statutes of the state. The generalization based on these cases is clearly to the effect that in most circumstances if a local board of education wishes to add something to the curriculum, and the item is not barred by state law, the board has such implied power. In fact this doctrine is so firmly established that in recent times it has been rarely challenged directly. The objectors to the addition of new studies normally have been taxpayers whose concern was essentially financial. Other cases, however, have involved religious influences. Also the issue is often introduced as a supplemental one in cases involving requiring pupils to partake of some curricular activity.

The Supreme Court of Indiana in an early case treated the question as follows:

The power to establish graded schools carries with it, of course, the power to establish and enforce such reasonable rules as may seem necessary to the trustees, in their discretion, for the government and discipline of such schools, and prescribing the course of instruction therein.

It cannot be doubted, we think, that the legislature has given the trustees of the public school corporations the discretionary power to direct, from time to time, what branches of learning, in addition to those specified in the statute, shall be taught in the public schools of their respective corporations.[12]

Appellate courts have upheld the establishment by local boards of education, without mandate or express permission from the state legislature, of courses of instruction in such subjects as bookkeeping, dancing, debating, dramatics, drawing, languages (ancient and modern), music, physical education, and thrift (involving savings deposits in a bank).

CHANGING THE CURRICULUM

Occasionally the reverse of the situation just discussed arises—namely, a suit to prevent the board of education from dropping a course which is not mandated by the state but which has been offered locally. It is not suprising to find that the courts take the attitude that the implied powers of local boards permit deleting as well as adding courses at the discretion of the board. For example, the dropping of kindergartens during the depression years with consequent abolition of positions of teachers who taught in them has been judicially sustained.

Nor are school boards restricted in altering the curriculum to fit the needs as they see them. In upholding the dismissal of a teacher who was unable to teach in the new curriculum (commercial subjects) which had attracted students away from the program in which she had taught (traditional academic), a court said:

> It is the administrative function of the school directors and superintendents to meet changing educational conditions through the creation of new courses, reassignment of teachers, and rearrangement of curriculum.[13]

The reluctance of the courts to interfere with a board's discretion in this area was emphatically restated as recently as 1950 in these words:

> . . . the Board of Education has complete discretion to determine what courses shall be given, continued or discontinued and this cannot be controlled or interfered with by any court.[14]

SCOPE OF PROGRAM

Activities other than academic instruction have been challenged as being beyond the power of local boards to provide. A case in point arose in an unusual way in Kansas. The case was instituted by the state tax commission, which claimed that state sales tax should be paid on activities sponsored by the local board for which an admissions fee was charged, because the activities allegedly were not a bona fide part of the curriculum. The court did not sustain the claim. Activities which the Supreme Court of Kansas supported since "the Board of Education has concluded they are a part of its educational program" included athletic contests, musical recitals, dramatics, dances, and lectures. It stated:

> School boards and boards of education have authority to provide for instruction in subjects other than those required to be taught by the statutes or by courses of study prescribed by the state board of education, and in so doing may exercise a discretion with which the courts may not interfere, unless a clear case of fraud or abuse is shown.[15]

The added costs inherent in comprehensive physical education programs have led to a substantial number of cases in this area. The courts have gone quite far, however, in the face of considerable protest in permitting local boards to determine the elements of a good physical education program. The Supreme Court of Montana reasoned as follows on the issue:

> Mentality without physical well-being does not make for good citizenship—the good citizen, the man or woman who is of the greatest value to the state, is the one whose every faculty is developed and alert.[16]

Since training for citizenship was considered to be the primary purpose of the public schools, the court sustained the building and equipping of an outdoor "gymnasium." In an Arizona case involving the building of a stadium which would be used to a great extent for competitive games, the power of the board to spend money for the stadium was upheld in an opinion which included this language regarding competitive athletics:

> It seems to us that, to hold things of this kind are less fitted for the ultimate purpose of our public schools, to wit, the making of good citizens, physically, mentally, and morally, than the study of algebra and Latin, is an absurdity. Competitive athletic games, therefore, from every standpoint, may properly be included in a public school curriculum.[17]

Health programs established by local boards of education have been another source of considerable litigation. It is clear that school boards have the authority to require pupils to meet reasonable health standards as a condition of school attendance. Beyond this, however, the courts have had to consider how far boards of education can go in providing health services.

One aspect of the problem involves the question of whether, in the absence of express legislative authority, a local board may employ doctors, dentists, and nurses to inspect the children to see that health requirements are met. One court has spoken on the matter as follows:

> The power of the school board to exclude pupils who do not meet reasonable health requirements, which is undoubted, necessitates the conclusion that they have the power:
>
> (1) To make the requirements, and therefore to take expert advice as to what those requirements ought to be.
>
> (2) To determine whether the pupil meets them, which requires expert advice and inspection, therefore they may employ suitable persons to give advice and make such inspection.[18]

The philosophy of the issue has been well stated by another court in the following words:

> The purpose of the . . . [district] is to maintain efficient free public schools . . . and, unless expressly restricted, [it] necessarily possesses the power to employ such persons as are required to accomplish that purpose. Education of a child means much more than merely communicating to it the contents of textbooks. But even if the term were to be so limited, some discretion must be used by the teacher in determining the amount of study each child is capable of. The physical and mental powers of the individual are so interdependent that no system of education, although designed solely to develop mentality, would be complete which ignored bodily health.[19]

There is, however, a limit to providing health services by boards of education. School health programs may not include medical or surgical treatments for disease. Maintenance of a clinic, where medical and dental treatment was given pupils of the district at district expense when the children's parents were unable to pay for it, has been held beyond the implied powers of local boards.[20] Of necessity, local boards "must be deemed to have implied authority to assume responsibility for first aid, medical or surgical services rendered to a pupil who is injured or becomes ill while engaged in school activities," according to one court. This court held, however, that such implied authority did not include payment for the services of an attending physician after the emergency.[21]

METHODS OF INSTRUCTION

In General

If a statute treats the methodology to be employed in teaching some subject, this must be observed locally. Almost all states have some laws which impinge on methodology, but most prescriptions tend to be general and suggestive rather than specific and exclusive. Thus, in general, determination of methods is essentially a local, rather than a state, decision.

The courts recognize the common-sense need for placing the responsibility for method on the local board rather than on parents or the courts. A taxpayer's complaint that a local board was having book-keeping taught by the single entry method when the double entry was the correct way in his opinion, was dismissed by an Iowa court, which, in refusing to interfere, said that "selection of the books to be used, the methods employed and the character of the instruction suitable for the pupils is an exercise of discretion" by the board.[22] It has been the prevailing attitude of courts in general not to interfere with the methods required or permitted by school authorities.

Occasionally, however, it is with obvious reluctance that a court refrains from ruling that a procedure is unreasonable, as when a court held that "the management and direction of pupils and studies" was out of its jurisdiction in a case involving a parent's complaint that her child's health had been injured from anxiety over a teacher's assigning a student in the class to grade papers, the student marker often erroneously grading the paper of the complainant's son. But the court said further:

> While constrained to the decision we cannot refrain from the expression of disapproval of the practice of setting a rival pupil in judgment upon the work of an eager and zealous competitor.[23]

The relationship between the board of education and the professional staff in the matter of methods was discussed by the highest court of West Virginia as follows:

> The law does not contemplate that the members of a board of education shall supervise the professional work of teachers, principals, and superintendents. They are not teachers, and ordinarily, not qualified to be such. Generally they do not possess qualifications to pass upon methods of instruction and discipline. The law clearly contemplated that professionally

trained teachers, principals and superintendents shall have exclusive control of these matters.

This comment was made in a case pertaining to the attempted dismissal of a county superintendent who had had a "clash" with "some unnamed member of the board on some unstated pedagogical questions."[24]

Textbooks and Materials

There is no question as to the legal right of the state to prescribe textbooks. It was succinctly stated in 1899 by one court in a leading case:

> That the State may establish a uniform series of books to be taught in the schools, which it provides and controls, seems to be a proposition as evident as that it may provide a uniform system of schools, which we take it is not now an open question. . . .[25]

All states have some statutes pertaining to textbooks, and many have detailed prescriptions in this area. The laws pertain to such items as establishment of state-approved lists of books, free textbooks, conditions under which textbooks can be changed (e.g., not more frequently than every five years, with possible exceptions), material to be included in textbooks (e.g., effects of alcohol and narcotics), proscribed material (e.g., sectarian doctrines), and conditions under which publishers may sell books in the state (e.g., charging prices no higher than in other jurisdictions). In some states local boards have almost unlimited power in regard to textbook selection, whereas in other states their freedom of choice is restricted to lists of books approved by the state, the lists varying widely in regard to number of approved books per subject. There are differences in several states between procedures for elementary grades and those for high school, or among procedures for different subjects offered.

Generally, supplementary books and instructional materials may be purchased at the discretion of the local board if it deems the items necessary for the proper conduct of a course. On the whole, courts have sustained boards in their determinations of such matters.

Frequently, there are attempts by voters in a district to have a particular book removed from the schools. The post-World War II period has been one of considerable agitation in this area. The most frequent complaints involve "un-American teachings," loosely defined. Another common charge is that a particular volume portrays some group in an unfairly unfavorable light. While a local board may wish to accede to such requests or demands for removal of books, legally it cannot be forced to remove a book which in its discretion is deemed appropriate. Obviously, a school board has the implied duty, if it does not have the express obligation, to prevent teaching of subversive doctrines and to see that false ideas of superiority or inferiority of various groups in our democracy are not conveyed to pupils. The standard in regard to legal acceptability of books for use in public schools has been set by one court in a case where it was sought to remove *The Merchant of Venice* and *Oliver Twist* from use in high school classes as follows:

> Except where a book has been maliciously written for the apparent purpose of promoting and fomenting a bigoted and intolerant hatred against a particular racial or religious group, public interest in a free and democratic society does not warrant or encourage the suppression of any book at the whim of any unduly sensitive person or group of persons, merely because a character described in such book belonging to a particular race or religion is portrayed in a derogatory or offensive manner. The necessity for the suppression of such a book must clearly depend upon the intent and motive which has actuated the author in making such a portrayal.[26]

CONSTITUTIONAL PROBLEMS

Moral and Spiritual Values

It should be pointed out that some methods adopted in good faith to accomplish desirable ends may be in violation of the federal or state constitution. It has already been noted that in a few jurisdictions Bible-reading has been judicially barred; but this is not the situation in most states. The same observation may be made relative to offering the Lord's Prayer in school. There is less consistency in the state rulings regarding the singing of religious hymns.[27] The United States Supreme Court has never ruled on these issues. In 1952, however, that court dismissed for want of jurisdiction an appeal from a judgment of the Supreme Court of New Jersey sustaining a statute providing for the reading, without comment, of five verses from the Old Testament at the opening of each school day. In this case, the action of a parent, based on an alleged violation of his child's rights under the First Amendment, had become moot since the child had been graduated during the period of litigation.[28]

In regard to the methods employed by boards of education to incorporate moral and spiritual attitudes in the curriculum, two United States Supreme Court decisions are applicable. In 1948 the court disapproved, as being in violation of the prescription of the First Amendment regarding freedom of religion and the "due process" clause of the Fourteenth Amendment, a plan adopted by the school board of Champaign, Illinois. The plan involved the permitting of religious instruction in school buildings during school hours on an optional basis. The Champaign Council on Religious Education was formed by members of the Jewish, Roman Catholic, and some Protestant faiths. The Council employed the teachers at no expense to the school board. The instructors, however, were subject to the approval and general supervision of the superintendent of schools. These teachers of religion taught for forty-five minutes a week those students whose parents had signed request cards for this purpose. Children taking the religious instruction of their faith were required to attend these classes as they would be required to attend other classes. Those not participating went to another part of the building to continue secular studies. The Supreme Court of Illinois had upheld the plan, but the judgment was reversed by the United States Supreme Court, which found:

> The operation of the State's compulsory education system thus assists and is integrated with the program of religious instruction carried on by separate religious sects. Pupils compelled by law to go to school for secular education are released in part from their legal duty upon the condition that they attend the religious classes. This is beyond all question a utilization of the tax-established and tax-supported public school system to aid religious groups to spread their faith. And it falls squarely under the ban of the First Amendment (made applicable to the States by the Fourteenth). . . .

The court emphasized specifically a ban on the use of tax-supported school buildings for such purposes.[29]

Four years later, however, the United States Supreme Court approved a method adopted by the New York City Board of Education. This plan provided "released time" of one hour on one afternoon a week for those pupils whose parents requested that they be excused to attend religious instruction off the school premises. The opinion of the court distinguished this case from the Illinois case essentially on the points that school facilities here were not used and that the administrative machinery of the schools was not substantially involved in the program (no approval or supervision of teachers and no comment by school personnel on attendance or nonattendance of pupils). In the words of the court:

> In the McCollum case the classrooms were used for religious instruction and the force of the public school was used to promote that instruction. Here, as we have said, the public schools do no more than accommodate their schedules to a program of outside religious instruction. We follow the McCollum case. But we cannot expand it to cover the present released time program unless separation of Church and State means that public institutions can make no adjustment of their schedules to accommodate the religious needs of the people. We cannot read into the Bill of Rights such a philosophy of hostility to religion.

Three of the Justices dissented from this opinion.[30]

Patriotism

Another method designed to accomplish a desirable end was barred by the United States Supreme Court when it held that the flag salute was not an acceptable way of teaching patriotism if a pupil or his parent objected to this observance. Although this case involved a regulation of a state board of education, the holding overruled a previous one sustaining the right of a local board to require the flag salute and pledge of allegiance. The opinion included the following frequently quoted passage:

> If there is any fixed star in our constitutional constellation, it is that no official, high or petty, can prescribe what shall be orthodox in politics, nationalism, religion, or other matters of opinion or force citizens to confess by word or act their faith therein. If there are any circumstances which permit an exception, they do not now occur to us.[31]

Requiring Pupils to Study a Subject (Parent's Right to Choose)

The flag salute case points up the necessity of clearly differentiating between the power of a school board to put something in the curriculum and the power to require that every student partake of the experience. The United States Supreme Court did not ban the use of the flag salute in the curriculum; it did bar the forcing of every child to submit to the activity. The conflict is between the rights of the government (the local school board being a part of the government) in relation to the education of its citizens and the rights of parents in relation to the education of their children.

Some generalizations as to the legal pattern in this area have been set out carefully by the Supreme Court of Colorado (incorporating several United States Supreme Court decisions) as follows:

> The powers of the State, the children and their parents over their education may be briefly but accurately stated thus:
> 1. The state, for its own protection, may require children to be educated. . . .
> 2. Certain studies plainly essential to good citizenship must be taught. . . . And, as a corollary, such studies may be required of every child.
> 3. Liberty is more than freedom from imprisonment. . . . The right to conduct a private school; the right of parents to have their children taught where, when, how, what, and by whom they may judge best, are among the liberties guaranteed by section I of the Fourteenth Amendment of the United States Constitution. . . .
> 4. But these rights are subject to the qualifications 1 and 2, above, and that teachers and places must be reputable and the things taught not immoral or inimical to the public welfare. . . .
> 5. Conversely, the teaching of what is immoral or inimical to the public welfare may be forbidden by the state, even though taught as a moral and religious duty, e.g., polygamy. . . .
>
> It necessarily follows that if parents can have their children taught what they please, they can refuse to have them taught what they think harmful, barring what must be taught; i.e., the essentials of good citizenship. What these are the board of education of each district, primarily, and the courts ultimately, must decide. So whether any study is immoral or inimical to the public welfare the board primarily and the courts ultimately must decide.[32]

Thus, a student may be required to pursue any course which could be shown to be "essential to good citizenship" regardless of the will of his parents. In this connection it is pertinent to recall the flag salute decision of the United States Supreme Court, which decision was subsequent to the above statement. There the high tribunal deemed the flag salute and pledge of allegiance not so necessary to the inculcation of good citizenship as to warrant its requirement when a parent objected on religious grounds. The difficulty confronting a school board in trying to prove a subject absolutely essential to the accomplishment of the purpose of the schools is apparent.

Another consideration involved when a child refuses to take a course is whether the parent has expressly instructed the child not to do so. If the refusal is not based on the instructions of the parent, it seems well settled that the pupil is subject to disciplinary measures adopted by the board to include suspension or expulsion. This is true also if the parent has instructed the child but will give no reason for the stand.

If a constitutional right is substantially involved, however, in the reason of the parent, for example, religious scruples, the courts will uphold the parent. This was the situation in the flag salute case. It is intrinsically woven into many other decisions, such as the Bible-reading cases where frequently it has been held that while laws or board rules requiring Bible-reading without comment are not in violation of most state constitutions, the forcing of a pupil to participate against his parent's religious reasons would be prohibited. In several cases, specific comments have been made by courts to the effect that rights of religious liberty are not violated if attendance upon the exercise is optional.[33] Some courts, however, have upheld the legality of Bible-reading without considering the issue of required attendance when that issue was not squarely brought before them.[34]

In order to sustain a claim of religious grounds as a reason for having a child excused from a course, it has been held not necessary that the parent be affiliated with a religious organization opposed to the activity, because the Constitution makes a person's religious beliefs personal.[35] In regard to constitutional grounds, one court has gone so far as to hold that:

> . . . the right of parents to select, within limits, what their children shall learn, is one of the liberties guaranteed by the Fourteenth Amendment to the national Constitution, and of which, therefore, no state can deprive them.[36]

This reasoning is an extension of the common law principle giving the father control over the education of his child. Also, it is predicated on the reasonableness of the parental choice.

What constitutes a reasonable selection of courses by a parent has been the source of much litigation. While there are exceptions, an analysis of the cases leads to the generalization that the courts tend to support almost any reason presented without ulterior motives or intentions. As one court has said, "If a reasonable request is made by a parent, it should be heeded." In that instance a parent did not want his daughter to take the required course in domestic science. Rather, he wanted her to spend the time required for that class, and for the travel to the separate building where the class was held, in taking private music lessons. The court thought this a reasonable determination by the parent and binding on school authorities.[37]

Perhaps the extreme to which a court has gone in sustaining a parent's right to select his child's subjects of study was when the Supreme Court of Nebraska accepted as a justifiable reason for refusing to allow his child to study grammar the parent's contention "that said study was not taught in said school as he had been instructed when he went to school." The court there held:

> The right of the parent ... to determine what studies his child shall pursue is paramount to that of the trustees or teacher. . . . No pupil attending the school can be compelled to study any prescribed branch against the protest of the parent ... so long as the failure of the ... [pupil to do so] does not prejudice the equal rights of other students. . . .[38]

It should be noted that the court considered the factor of whether the excusing of a child from participation in an exercise or study will interfere with the rights of other children. The same point is made in the following frequently quoted words of another court in an old case:

> No parent has the right to demand that the interests of the children of others shall be sacrificed for the interests of his child; and he cannot, consequently, insist that his child shall be placed or kept in particular classes, when by so doing others will be retarded in the advancement they would otherwise make; or that his child shall be taught studies not in the prescribed course of the school, or be allowed to use a text-book different from that decided to be used in the school, or that he shall be allowed to adopt methods of study that interfere with others in their studies. The rights of each are to be enjoyed and exercised only with reference to the equal rights of all others.[39]

It seems well settled that school authorities have the power to set up reasonable requirements as to proficiency required for acceptance in a course, retention in a course, promotion, and obtaining a diploma. The distinction between excluding a pupil from a given class and expelling him from school because of lack of proficiency is an important one. The former power is necessary to the general conduct and orderly operation of the schools; the latter is in conflict with compulsory education laws.

CITATIONS

1. Talbot v. Board of Education, 14 N.Y.S.2d 340 (1939).
2. Ring v. City of Woburn, 311 Mass. 679, 43 N.E.2d 8 (1942).
3. School Commissioners v. State, 129 Ind. 14, 28 N.E. 61 (1891).
4. State *ex rel.* Mueller v. Common School Board, 208 Wis. 257, 242 N.W. 574 (1932).
5. Prevey v. School District No. 6, 263 Mich. 622, 249 N.W. 15 (1933).
6. Wagner v. Royal, 36 Wash. 428, 78 P. 1094 (1904).
7. State *ex rel.* Dearle v. Frazier, 102 Wash. 369, 173 P. 35 (1918).
8. Meyer v. Nebraska, 262 U.S. 390, 43 S.Ct. 625 (1923).
9. Stuart v. School District No. 1 of Kalamazoo, 30 Mich. 69 (1874).
10. *Cf.* Zimmerman v. Board of Education, 199 N.C. 259, 154 S.E. 397 (1930), and Wyatt v. Harrison, 177 Miss. 13, 170 So. 526 (1936).
11. State v. Ghrist, 222 Ia. 1069, 270 N.W. 376 (1936).
12. State *ex rel.* Andrews v. Webber, 108 Ind. 31, 8 N.E. 708 (1886).
13. Jones v. Holes, 334 Pa. 538, 6 A.2d 102 (1939).
14. State *ex rel.* Brewton v. Board of Education of St. Louis, 361 Mo. 86, 233 S.W.2d 697 (1950).
15. State Tax Commission v. Board of Education of Holton, 146 Kan. 722, 73 P.2d 49 (1937).
16. McNair v. School District No. 1, 87 Mont. 423, 288 P.188 (1930).
17. Alexander v. Phillips, 31 Ariz. 503, 254 P. 1056 (1927).
18. Hallett v. Post Printing and Publishing Company, 68 Colo. 573, 192 P. 919 (1920).
19. State *ex rel.* Stoltenberg v. Brown, 112 Minn. 370, 128 N.W. 294 (1910).
20. McGilvra v. Seattle School District, 113 Wash. 619, 194 P. 817 (1921).
21. Jarrett v. Goodall, 113 W. Va. 478, 168 S.E. 763 (1933).
22. Neilan v. Board of Directors, 200 Ia. 860, 205 N.W. 506 (1925).
23. Wulff v. Inhabitants of Wakefield, 221 Mass. 427, 109 N.E. 358 (1915).
24. State *ex rel.* Rogers v. Board of Education of Lewis County, 125 W. Va. 579, 25 S.E.2d 537 (1943).
25. Leeper v. State of Tennessee, 103 Tenn. 500, 53 S.W. 962 (1899).
26. Rosenberg v. Board of Education of City of New York, 196 Misc. 542, 92 N.Y.S.2d 344 (1949).

27. *Cf.* Moore v. Monroe, 64 Ia. 367, 20 N.W. 475 (1884); and State *ex rel.* Freeman v. Scheve, 65 Neb. 853, 91 N.W. 846 (1902).

28. Doremus v. Board of Education, 342 U.S. 429, 72 S.Ct. 394 (1952).

29. Illinois *ex rel.* McCollum v. Board of Education of Champaign, 333 U.S. 203, 68 S.Ct. 461 (1948).

30. Zorach v. Clauson, 343 U.S. 306, 72 S.Ct. 679 (1952).

31. West Virginia State Board of Education v. Barnette, 319 U.S. 624, 63 S.Ct. 1178 (1943).

32. People *ex rel.* Vollmar v. Stanley, 81 Colo. 276, 255 P. 610 (1927).

33. Doremus v. Board of Education, 5 N.J. 435, 75 A.2d 880 (1950).

34. Carden v. Bland, 288 S.W.2d 718 (Tenn. 1956).

35. Hardwick v. Board of School Trustees of Fruitridge, 54 Cal. App. 696, 205 P. 49 (1921).

36. People *ex rel.* Vollmar v. Stanley, *supra* note 32.

37. State *ex rel.* Kelley v. Ferguson, 95 Neb. 63, 144 N.W. 1039 (1914).

38. State *ex rel.* Sheibley v. School District No. 1, 31 Neb. 552, 48 N.W. 393 (1891).

39. Trustees of Schools v. People *ex rel.* Van Allen, 87 Ill. 303 (1877).

IV

THE AUTHORITY OF SCHOOL BOARDS
IN RELATION TO EMPLOYED PERSONNEL

IN GENERAL

The authority of local boards of education in respect to employed personnel of the school system constitutes an especially active area of litigation. The entire gamut of personnel policies and practices from initial employment, through working conditions in service, to retirement must be taken into account. There is in this area a marked trend toward increased state-level regulation through statutes which mandate certain procedures with which local boards must comply (e.g., tenure laws) or which set up minimum standards and requirements below which local boards may not go (e.g., salary laws). Also there is a trend toward the enactment of permissive legislation which expressly authorizes local boards to do certain things about which previously there had been a question of implied power —such things for example, as covering teachers under workmen's compensation laws. In one sense, the power of local boards is somewhat circumscribed by such statutes. In another, however, boards are being given guideposts, presumably based on insight and tested experience, in areas previously essentially uncharted. There are, of course, wide variations among the states in regard to the scope of legislation affecting personnel within local school districts. Operation of a local school system is so complex, however, and local autonomy is so cherished a concept in the general legal pattern of American education, that local boards still are vested with broad discretionary powers in the implementation of the state legal provisions.

EMPLOYMENT

Local boards of education have the power to select teachers under such reasonable rules as they may adopt, subject to constitutional and statutory restrictions. Every state has established certification requirements for teachers, and no board can employ a teacher who does not meet the standards of licensure. It should be noted that statutory and judicial interpretations vary on the implementation of this principle. In some states a contract with an uncertificated teacher is void, that is, a contract cannot be made. In others a teacher must have the certificate before he actually begins to teach. In still others the stipulation is that no salary can be paid an uncertificated teacher. It is the responsibility of the board to be certain the teacher is certificated at the proper time. Teachers' contracts are discussed in Chapter VII.

There is no constitutional right to be employed just because one has the necessary license. Boards of education may establish reasonable qualifications for teachers beyond those required by the state for certification. Use of professional examinations by local boards to determine fitness of teachers has been judicially approved. So has a local requirement that teachers pass a physical examination. Likewise rules requiring statements related to loyalty of applicants have been sustained.

However, some rules regarding employment of teachers clearly would come under constitutional or statutory bars in most states. For example, religious or political tests applied to teacher applicants would be beyond the power of a board to apply. Many other rules are subject to attack. It must be borne in mind, however, that an unwise rule cannot be struck down by a court, and there is often a tremendous difference between an unwise and an illegal rule.

Board rules against the employment of married women teachers have on several occasions, including some recent decisions, been sustained in the absence of prohibitive statutes.[1] Also upheld by courts in three states have been rules against employing teachers who are affiliated with a labor union. In the words of the Supreme Court of Illinois:

> The board has the absolute right to decline to employ or to reemploy any applicant for any reason whatever or for no reason at all. The board is responsible for its action only to the people of the city, from whom, through the mayor, the members have received their appointments. It is no infringement upon the constitutional rights of any one for the board

to decline to employ him as a teacher in the schools, and it is immaterial whether the reason for the refusal to employ him is because the applicant is married or unmarried, is of fair complexion or dark, is or is not a member of a trades union, or whether no reason is given for such refusal. The board is not bound to give any reason for its action. It is free to contract with whomsoever it chooses.[2]

SALARY

Bases of Classification

In the absence of state laws or in conjunction with state laws local boards of education have wide discretion in the matter of determination of employees' salaries. So long as they comply with pertinent statutes, boards may utilize any method of assigning salaries that is "reasonable, natural, and based upon substantial difference germane to the subject, or upon some basis having a reasonable relation to the work assigned."[3]

Courts, when involved in interpreting salary schedules, do not give attention to the wisdom of the classifications, but only to any alleged arbitrariness in the classifications or the administration of the schedule. The Supreme Court of California has stated the general principle as follows:

> It must be conceded that, within the limits fixed by the School Code, the Board has discretionary control over the salaries of the teachers. . . . However, it must also be conceded that the legislature has enjoined on such Boards, within reasonable limits, the principle of uniformity of treatment as to salary for those performing like services with like experience. . . . This limitation, however, does not prevent the Board from making reasonable classifications.[4]

It seems clear that there is no legal bar to a school board's setting up salary classifications provided they are on reasonable bases and are not administered in a discriminatory manner. Recently in Minnesota the Supreme Court of that state sustained a determination by a local board of a large city that teachers in a special vocational-technical school should be a class treated differently from teachers of vocational subjects in the regular secondary schools on the basis that qualifications of the two classes of teachers differed.[5]

On the issue of classifying teachers for salary purposes on the basis of race, the cases are in agreement that such action falls under the ban of "both the due process and the equal protection clauses of the Fourteenth Amendment."[6]

In placing teachers new to the school system on the salary schedule, it is the prerogative of the board to evaluate outside experience. One court which dealt in detail with this subject held that a local board did not need to grant any credit for experience outside the system. If it did grant credit, it could do so on the basis of an examination of each individual case, or according to fixed rules, or by a combination of the two methods. Once it has a policy, however, the policy would have to be administered fairly and without discrimination.[7]

The "Merit" Factor

Courts have not interpreted the principle of uniformity to mean absolute sameness. Recognition of individual differences is not precluded. For example, a school system had a schedule providing periodic salary increases to teachers who earned additional college credits during each four years of employment and reductions for those who did not obtain such credits. This plan was held to be a reasonable, and therefore legal, classification. The court summarized a number of decisions in its opinion as follows:

> . . . a board of education may exercise its discretion in adopting salary schedules fixing the compensation to be paid to permanent teachers although (1) the schedule must be adopted prior to the beginning of the school year; (2) any allowance based upon years of training and experience must be uniform, and subject to reasonable classification; and (3) the schedule must not be arbitrary, discriminatory or unreasonable.[8]

In another case the following statement was made by the Supreme Court of California:

> It is quite possible that a situation might exist in which one of two teachers of similar experience and service might be not only more capable, but also more industrious and willing than the other, who although sufficiently competent to prohibit dismissal, might be somewhat indolent and non-cooperative. In such a situation the school board should be permitted to exercise its reasonable discretion in raising the salary of the industrious teacher as a reward for her good work without at the same time having to increase the salary of the undeserving teacher.

In this case, however, the court made it clear that an alleged use of subjective standards cannot justify discriminatory action against teachers for other reasons. The situation was one in which the salaries of two teachers were reduced, allegedly because, in the words of the superintendent, they "didn't seem to embrace whole-heartedly the philosophy of teaching which I was trying to get over to them at the time." The teachers claimed the reason was to force them to resign and thereby sacrifice their tenure status. The court found for the teachers, and noted expressly the following:

> If such generalities were permitted to be used as justification for salary changes, then the actions of the administrative boards would not be discretionary but wholly arbitrary. The instant case is illustrative of the inadvisability of using such a method to test the value of a teacher.[9]

An example of a subjective method of determining teacher effectiveness, where unsatisfactory teachers did not get salary increases, was judicially upheld in 1950 in California. A committee consisting of the principal, two vice-principals, and the head of the teacher's department "evaluated the teacher's teaching effectiveness and educational worth by measuring her actual classroom performance against a number of factors, including personality, skill as an instructor, scholarship, ability to discipline, character building, professonial growth, professional loyalty, community interests and standing, power of expression oral and written, influence on pupils, tact and sympathy, initiative, persistence, energy, personal appearance and culture and refinement." The board acted on the recommendation of the committee. In sustaining this procedure, the court spoke as follows:

> The determination of the school board in the instant action that the salaries of teachers should be fixed for the years in question in accordance with the standard of satisfactoriness seems to us to be a reasonable one and therefore conclusive upon the court, and that the schedules are not discriminatory in their application to the petitioner as there was no reduction of the salary of teachers found to be unsatisfactory and teachers in such a class were all affected equally.[10]

The "Duties" Factor

The duties of a position rather than a title form the basis of reasonable classification. The highest court of Massachusetts has held that not all persons holding the rank of supervisor need be paid similarly. In a case in which a supervisor of arithmetic claimed she should be paid the same salary as a supervisor of manual training, the court, after looking at their duties, disagreed in these words:

> Supervision is the only common element in the work of the two teachers, and it is obvious that supervision of the work in manual training must differ substantially from supervision of the teaching of arithmetic.[11]

Often the question of salary reduction arises in connection with transfers to other assignments. The situation varies from state to state, with no consistent nationwide pattern apparent either in the statutes or judicial interpretations. In 1953 a Pennsylvania court gave the following ruling:

> . . . the abolition of a specially created office carries with it the abolition of the salary; and the Code does not prevent the last incumbent of the position from being returned to his former position with its attendant salary.[12]

In 1955 the Supreme Court of Louisiana treated the question of salary when a post is eliminated as follows:

> An honest discontinuance of his office does not automatically remove a permanent teacher from the school system. He remains therein and should forthwith be placed in a position of standing equal to that formerly held, if it be possible. In any event, he is nonetheless entitled to the salary attributable to the status he has attained even though he be reemployed in a position of lesser rank.[13]

If a teacher voluntarily assumes the duties of a position for which a higher salary schedule is provided, he is not thereby necessarily entitled to the higher salary. A case in point arose in New York City where a group of teachers who had been assigned as department chairmen without increases in pay brought suit to obtain the additional salary provided on the schedule for department chairmen. Actually only one of the fifty-four teachers involved held a chairman's license. The teachers alleged that the board did not hold examinations for this license and therefore they could not qualify. The court held, however, that even if the board should have given examinations, the fact that it had not done so did not place the complaining teachers in the same position as if they had passed the examination required for the chairman's license. The court denounced the board's practice as a "subterfuge which . . . is morally wrong and scholastically hazardous," but it dismissed the teachers' suit with the following holding:

> Our courts have unvaryingly adhered to the principle that a teacher who performs the duty of a higher grade until that grade is finally filled as provided by law is not entitled to the . . . salary attached to it.[14]

Judicial approval has been given to plans providing "extra pay for extra work." Supplemental contracts to cover extra duties have been treated by one court in the following words:

> Where the service is not part of the duties of the teacher, there is nothing to prevent the board from arranging for such extra service and paying for the same. . . .[15]

Sex and Dependency Factors

About one third of the states have laws expressly prohibiting salary differentiations on the basis of sex. These are the so-called "equal pay" laws. In 1952 in Massachusetts, which has a law of this type, a question arose as to the legality of "dependency allowances," that is, extra payments to married teachers who were the sole support of a spouse, a child, or children. The amount in this instance was $300 per year. The Supreme Judicial Court of Massachusetts refused to void the resolution, saying:

> If the vote [to grant dependency allowances] is to be held valid it must be because the committee could reasonably believe that it would be for the good of the school system to pay more for teachers having dependents. . . . On the whole, we incline to the view that the . . . [allowance] can be sustained. It is not that married teachers with dependents are for that reason likely to be better teachers than other persons—a proposition which it might be difficult to maintain. Rather the reason is that in a time when . . . the securing of the most competent teachers for the public schools has become a considerable problem, . . . it may be thought with some justification that the more mature, experienced, and competent teachers are those most likely to be married and to have dependents, and that some recognition of the additional burden which such teachers carry will have some effect in the long run in securing and in retaining for the public schools the services of teachers of that type.[16]

This reasoning is in line with the general proposition that any distinctions in salary based on personal factors must, in order to be judicially approved, relate the factors reasonably to legitimate school purposes. The courts are divided, however, on the question of whether marriage can be used as a basis for determining compensation for female teachers. A negative answer was given by the Supreme Court of Indiana, the opinion including this statement:

> The compensation of . . . [the female teacher] was fixed by the board, partly at least upon the fact that she was married. This, in our judgment, was unlawful and arbitrary, and formed no rational basis for a classification. It had no reasonable relation to the work assigned to her, as the fact that appellant was a married woman did not affect her ability to impart knowledge or perform her duties in the schoolroom.[17]

On the other hand, the Supreme Court of New Jersey has held as follows:

> There is no statute brought to our attention which requires the local board to fix any specified sum as salary for a teacher. It is entirely in the discretion of the local board. . . . Nor is there any statute prohibiting discrimination in the fixing of salaries as between married and unmarried teachers. There is a prohibition, as stated, against discrimination by reason of sex. In . . . [an earlier New Jersey case] it was said: ". . . we cannot say, even though they dismissed married or nonresident women teachers, giving preference in continued employment to residents of the school district and to those who would normally be dependent upon themselves for livelihood, that such action was an abuse of discretion or evidence of bad faith."[18]

Employees' Salary Rights

The adoption by a board of a salary schedule does not create a contract between the board and a teacher and vest the teacher with the right to be paid the increments announced. The prospective modification of a schedule is within the power of the board. As stated by one court:

> A regulation providing for increments is a mere declaration of legislative policy that is at all times subject to abrogation by the local board in the public interest.[19]

Reduction of salary is often covered by tenure laws where such exist. The general rule, to be discussed in more detail in the section "Dismissal," is that most tenure laws too are legislative policy declarations which can be modified by subsequent legislatures. Thus, the reduction of salaries of all teachers in a nondiscriminatory way has been upheld by courts. The United States Supreme Court found this permissible in a case where certain New Jersey teachers unsuccessfully claimed that their salaries could not be reduced by a local board acting under a permissive statute because of conflict with the tenure law, which they maintained prohibited any reductions in salary without following tenure procedure. The opinion in that case included these words:

> We think it was reasonable and proper that the teachers employed by the board should be divided into classes for the application of the percentage reduction. All in a given class were treated alike. Incidental individual inequality resulting in some instances from the operation of the plan does not condemn it as an unreasonable or arbitrary method of dealing with the problem of general salary reductions or deny the equality guaranteed by the Fourteenth Amendment.[20]

For teachers serving under annual contracts, each contract contains a salary stipulation mutually agreed upon when the contract is signed. In the absence of specific legislation a board could legally offer a teacher for a given year a salary less than that of the previous year. It should be noted, however, that state minimum salary laws cannot be avoided by contract provisions. It has been recently held that a teacher may sue to recover the full salary to which he is entitled under a state minimum salary law even if he signed a contract to teach at a lower salary.[21]

Salary Supplements

The question of legality of supplements to teachers' regular salaries often arises. The different interpretations in different states regarding purchase of insurance for teachers and building residences for staff personnel are discussed in Chapter VI.

The providing of sums of money for transportation of teachers has been disapproved by the Supreme Court of Tennessee as an illegal supplement to teachers' salaries. The statute applicable to public school transportation was held not to include teachers and funds could not be raised for the purpose of providing this "fringe benefit" to teachers. Said the court:

> If the Legislature wants to provide teacher transportation, the Legislature should and must say so in unmistakable terms, otherwise it seems to us that it is very clear from past Acts of the Legislature and from just common knowledge that the Legislature has never yet nor does not mean in the instant case to provide teacher transportation.[22]

In several states there are constitutional or statutory provisions prohibiting extra payments by public bodies after a contract has been entered into and performed in whole or part. Even in the absence of such a provision aimed at preventing the giving away of public money, there is some uncertainty as to whether a public employee's salary can be raised during the period of a contract. Technically, the employing district would be contractually entitled to the services at the original salary agreed upon. To be certain an increase in salary during a contract period is legal, the original contract should be terminated by mutual consent and a new one entered into at the higher figure. As noted previously, the procedure of entering into supplemental contracts when extra work is involved is legally sound.

RETIREMENT

In General

There has been more legislation related to retirement than to any other personnel policy. Much of it has dealt with technicalities which have led to a substantial amount of litigation. A large number of cases have been resolved in the context of specific legislative provisions and fact situations so narrow as to make generalization impossible beyond the jurisdiction involved. Also, probably because the details of retirement systems are understood only by the relatively few individuals actuarially trained, a suprisingly large number of statutes on the subject are poorly drawn, a situation which invites legal complications. Indeed, the Supreme Court of Iowa has said:

> The cases show that the predominant cause of the large amount of litigation having to do with public employees' pension or retirement systems is because the legislation establishing them uniformly promises much more than can be accomplished. The taxes and other public moneys and the contributions of the employees designed to maintain the retirement fund seldom build up sufficient reserves to pay the disability or service retirement allowances during the life expectancies. The systems are seldom actuarially sound. It is usually several years before this is fully realized. And when attempts are then made to strengthen the plan and to put it on a sounder financial basis either by increasing the contributions, raising the retirement age, or decreasing the allowances, the beneficiaries feel that their rights, present or prospective, are being impaired, when in fact what they think they have lost or will lose, is something impossible to obtain under the plan.[23]

Changes in Retirement Systems

In the preceding case it was held that a board may make changes in a retirement system if they are necessary to strengthen the financial soundness of the system. This principle has been generally followed by courts. If it were not, whole retirement systems could well collapse with resultant chaos and hardship.

Another point considered by courts in cases where individual members of a retirement system object to a change in the system is whether the proposed change provides a "substantial substitute" for the plan being dropped. The Supreme Court of Iowa in 1955 considered a case where two teachers who had been members of a local retirement plan objected to the dissolution of the system in favor of a new state plan including federal social security. The court, in deciding against the teachers, said:

> The provisions of the federal social security system are more favorable to members and their dependents than were those of the local system. Under the circumstances the required change from the local to the social security system does not appear to have been harsh or unfair to plaintiffs, and benefits accruing to them and their dependents under social security should eventually exceed those to which they would have been entitled under the local system.

In this case the complaining teachers had not yet reached retirement age, and the court restated the generally accepted rule in regard to rights to retirement allowances by those not yet eligible to retire as follows:

> . . . such prospective rights are not vested or contract rights which may not be adversely affected by subsequent legislation or procedure.[24]

Actuarial adjustments, such as those to take into account increased life expectancy, are permitted even if some not yet retired members of the system thereby have reduced their anticipated monthly allowances based on a fixed contribution.[25]

Generally, courts will not permit the allowances of those already retired to be changed to their disadvantage. When a "substantial substitute" was provided, courts have sanctioned the change. However, a change which would eventually have cut off the allowance of a retired teacher was declared unconstitutional by the Supreme Court of Utah, which discussed the issue as follows:

The promise made to teachers that if they will serve the public faithfully for a certain number of years and make contributions to a retirement fund from their salary, they will receive an annuity after retiring, is illusory if the Legislature can at any time repeal the retirement act and leave retired teachers with nothing but their equitable share of the assets of the association. This court . . . [in another case] stated that when a person has accepted an offer of the State or of one of its agencies, and has met all the conditions thereof, the State or agency is bound to perform the contract the same as a private person must perform. That principle applies in this case.[26]

The one exception noted in the cases is a practical consideration— solvency of the system. Reductions on a nondiscriminatory basis forced by true unavailability of funds could be approved, as one court said, "so long as entire deprivation is not thereby attempted under the guise of regulation of the amount of compensation." [27]

Whether the teacher contributed to the system is another factor considered in relation to changes in retirement plans. Technically a benefit financed by the employer is called a "pension" and one financed by the contributions of the member is called an "annuity." A pension is a gratuity to which no rights accrue. Annuity, however, implies a contractual obligation, which cannot be impaired. The United States Supreme Court in 1937 held that unless a contract right was clear from the wording of the statute, the presumption would be against such intention. That case involved a number of Chicago teachers who unsuccessfully claimed that reductions in their retirement allowances were not permissible because the law setting up the system created vested rights for them. The statute originally setting up the plan had used the word "annuity" to describe what was technically a "pension," but the court looked at the nature of the arrangement, not the name describing it.[28]

If a teacher joins a joint-contributory retirement system voluntarily, contract rights generally are held to have been acquired. The Supreme Court of Montana, in a case involving the amount of refund due a teacher who left the system before retiring, found unconstitutional a law which purported to eliminate from such refunds interest payments which had been included in the basic statute setting up the retirement system the teacher voluntarily had joined. The court reasoned that a contract was formed because two elements were present: the teacher had contributed to the fund, and such contribution was voluntary.[29]

Since today all new regular teachers in every state must join the retirement system, such reasoning would lead to the conclusion that to insure contract rights the language of the statute must explicitly so state that intention.

Raising Allowances of Those Retired

The point of changing payment after performance of a contract, previously discussed under "Salary Supplements," arises frequently in connection with increasing retirement allowances of those already retired. Although the idea is commendable from a social point of view, legal complications arise since it involves additional compensation for services already rendered. Recently, however, the highest courts of Illinois and Wisconsin have sustained increased benefits to retired teachers on the basis that a moral obligation to do so existed and that the discharge of a moral obligation is a public use of public funds and is therefore permissible. The Supreme Court of Wisconsin had previously held illegal such payments based on gratitude for services performed. Its more recent opinion distinguished "moral obligation" from "gratuity," the former being "an obligation which, though lacking in any foundation cognizable in law, springs from a sense of justice and equity, . . . but not from a mere sense of doing benevolence or charity." [30]

LEAVES

Policies regarding leaves of absence are generally within the discretionary power of local boards. All or nearly all states, however, have some applicable statutes which permit or require that leaves of specified duration be granted for certain purposes, for example, for attendance at county-level workshops or for illness. Almost without exception the statutes set up minima with nothing specifically to prevent local boards from developing policies to extend or supplement the state-level provisions when the policies can be justified as being in the best interests of the school system. The board cannot, of course, give away public money. The Supreme Judicial Court of Massachusetts has used the following language in upholding the implied power of a local school board to adopt a rule providing for sick leave pay:

The power of the school committee to make reasonable rules and regulations concerning the government, discipline and management of the schools under their charge and the compensation and methods of determining the amount and terms of payment of teachers, subject to provisions established by the Legislature, is not open to question. . . . This general grant of authority . . . includes the subsidiary power to decide within reasonable limits whether, in order to promote efficiency and insure constancy of excellent service on the part of teachers, temporary absences without loss of pay shall be afforded them.[31]

In 1954 the Supreme Court of Pennsylvania required the board of education of Philadelphia to pay a teacher for leave for military service rendered during the school year under a statute which entitled all state employees to paid leave up to fifteen days for such service. The fact that the teacher was not required to perform any school duties during July and August did not relieve the board from paying him for such leave taken during the school year.[32]

There has been a considerable amount of litigation regarding rights of teachers after leaves, especially in regard to tenure, salary, or retirement rights. Usually such decisions are based on interpretations of the language of the applicable statutes, and generalizations do not evolve.

Sometimes a question arises regarding the power of a board to require a teacher to take a leave of absence. Where mental or physical disability is involved, it seems clear that such power exists. An Indiana court held that a compulsory leave could be enforced by a board on a teacher who became a candidate for political office. Included in the court's opinion was the following:

It will be conceded that he [the teacher] has the same privilege as any other citizen to become a candidate for public office. Such candidacy should not be and is not ground for cancellation of his contract as a permanent teacher. But anyone who has been a candidate recognizes that political activity is apt to interfere with one's usual vocation and this fact, independent of any possible involvement of the school system in political controversies, affords a sound reason for temporary severance of the candidate's connection with the schools. This rule, general in terms and applying to all teachers, does not to us seem such an unreasonable exercise of the board's powers as to warrant judicial interference. The board not the courts is charged with the duty of managing the school system and so long as it acts with fairness its decisions on matters within its discretion are not subject to judicial review.[33]

COLLECTIVE BARGAINING

The extent to which public employees in general and local school board employees specifically can engage in activities related to the process of collective bargaining as practiced in private employment has not been judicially determined in most jurisdictions. Earlier in this chapter under "Employment" it was pointed out that school board rules against the employment of teachers who belong to unions have been sustained. On the other hand it seems clear that public employees, including teachers, can maintain membership in associations organized along occupational lines unless specifically prohibited by statute or board rule. The problems today arise primarily in connection with such issues as whether school employees can strike and to what extent school boards can legally agree to negotiate with teachers' organizations.

In 1957 the Supreme Court of New Hampshire held a strike by public school teachers to be illegal in the absence of legislation expressly permitting the use of this labor weapon. The court concluded:

> There is no doubt that the Legislature is free to provide by statute that public employees may enforce their right to collective bargaining by arbitration or strike. . . . Absent such legislation the collective action of the school teachers in refusing to work for the city in order to obtain salary increases even though executed in a reasonable manner was subordinate to the right enjoyed by the city against a strike by its employees.
>
> It was therefore illegal and properly enjoined. . . . The injunction restrained the concerted action of the defendants and did not in any way impose on any individual an obligation to work against his will.[34]

The Supreme Court of Errors of Connecticut in 1951 rendered a declaratory judgment finding strikes by school employees to be illegal. In the words of that court:

> Under our system, the government is established by and run for all of the people, not for the benefit of any person or group. The profit motive, inherent in the principle of free enterprise, is absent. It should be the aim of every employee of the government to do his or her part to make it function as efficiently and economically as possible. The drastic remedy of the organized strike to enforce the demands of unions of governmental employees is in direct contravention of this principle.[35]

In another case the same court condemned the use of a threat of a strike to coerce a board of education to grant salary increases. It held:

> Upon the facts which the court has found, the position of the plaintiffs implicit in their demands is one which neither legally nor morally commends itself. To accomplish their purpose to coerce the board of education, the plaintiffs threatened to cease work in disregard of the express provisions of their contracts. This was illegal. So too was their further threat to resort to a strike to enforce their demands. . . . Neither by committing nor threatening to commit an illegal act or acts can one enhance his legal rights. . . . If the court . . . found that illegal conduct of the plaintiffs was the proximate cause of an increase granted to them by the board of education, in no event could a recommendation by the board of finance of an appropriation by the town to pay such an increase either render the plaintiffs' contracts therefor binding upon the town or warrant making an appropriation by it to provide for payment thereunder.[36]

In 1951, however, a Minnesota court refused to restrain a strike by public school custodial employees. Involved was a statute prohibiting state courts from issuing restraining orders or temporary injunctions to prevent persons from stopping work in a labor dispute unless they were firemen, policemen, or had duties relating to the public safety. The court held that under the statute it could not restrain a strike by this group of employees as it did not deem public safety to be involved.[37]

The matter of negotiations between school boards and associations of teachers has been treated by the highest court in Connecticut as follows:

> The statutes and private acts give broad powers to the . . . [board] with reference to educational matters and school management. . . . If it chooses to negotiate with the . . . [association] with regard to employment, salaries, grievances procedure and working conditions of its members, there is no statute, public or private, which forbids such negotiations. It is a matter of common knowledge that this is the method pursued in most school systems large enough to support a teachers' association in some form. It would seem to make no difference theoretically whether the negotiations are with a committee of the whole association or with individuals of small related groups, so long as any agreement made with the committee is confined to members of the association.

The court further held that while a general arbitration agreement would be invalid in that power of the board would be illegally delegated, there is "no reason to deny the . . . [school board] the power to enter voluntarily into a contract to arbitrate a specific dispute" with the stipulation that the board's "power to submit to arbitration would not extend to questions of policy."[38]

DISMISSAL

In General

Conditions under which a school employee can be removed from his position are essentially governed by the provisions of his employment contract with the local board and by applicable state laws. It bears reiteration here that all pertinent state-level prescriptions as well as regulations of the local board are considered part of the contract. Also, the distinction should be made between failure to renew a contract which has expired and discharge of an employee during a contract period or under a tenure law. In regard to nonrenewal of a contract, an employee would have no legal redress unless an applicable statute were violated, which only rarely would be the case. Considerations involved in discharges are discussed below.

Under Differing Employment Conditions

Term Contracts. Where discharge is during the life of a contract, general contract law as discussed in Chapter VII would apply. The common law recognizes the authority of a school board to discharge an employee during a contract period for sufficient cause. Exactly what constitutes sufficient cause cannot be stated categorically. The school board has the burden of proof in showing that it is acting in the best interests of the system in removing a teacher under contract. In one of the leading cases on the point, the Supreme Court of Indiana discussed the situation in the following language:

> Now, if a teacher, although he has been employed for a definite length of time, proves to be incompetent, and unable to teach the branches of instruction he has been employed to teach, either from a lack of learning, or from an utter want of capacity to impart his learning to others; or if in any other respect, he fails to perform the obligations resting upon him as such teacher, whether arising from the express terms of his contract or by necessary implication, he has broken the agreement on his part, and the trustees are clearly authorized to dismiss him from such employment.[39]

Continuing Contracts. Many school districts operate under so-called continuing contract laws. Such statutes provide that if a board plans not to re-employ a teacher for a succeeding school year, he must be notified before a specified date during the current school year. The date usually is in the spring and often such contracts are referred to as "spring notification" contracts. In the event that the spring notification is not made, the contract is deemed in force for the next school year. Some statutes include details on what the notice must contain and how it should be delivered. If all procedures stipulated are observed, however, a teacher receiving notification has no redress under a continuing contract arrangement. The right of the teacher to prior notice of nonretention is essentially the only difference between a term contract and a continuing contract. Unfortunately, there is considerable semantic confusion among board members, educators, and lawyers involving continuing contract laws and tenure laws. The terms are often erroneously used a synonyms, but the differences legally are very significant. Thus the provisions of the statute, not the descriptive words, must be examined.

Tenure. Tenure statutes provide, with varying degrees of specificity, for a procedure which must be followed before a teacher entitled to tenure rights may be dismissed. A true tenure procedure has four distinct elements, three of which must be explicit in the statute, the fourth being reasonably implied from the first three.

The first element is notice to the employee that dismissal is being contemplated. Some statutes are quite detailed on this point. In any event, the notice must be received by the teacher a sufficient time before the hearing to enable him to prepare his defense.

The second element is a statement of the charges. These must be presented with enough specificity to enable the teacher to defend against them. Also they must be charges which, if proved, would constitute legal grounds for dismissal. Most tenure statutes list as reasons for dismissal such causes as incompetence, immorality, neglect of duty, and insubordination. Often an additional phrase like "other good cause" is appended to the list. In the absence of such a phrase, the courts generally require that the charges fit one or more of the specified categories of proscribed conduct. It is a rule of statutory construction that if the legislature lists grounds for dismissal it is assumed that the listing is all-inclusive unless there is evidence to the contrary.

The third element is a hearing. There the teacher should have a chance to defend himself against the charges. Usually the initial hearing is held before the local board of education. Even when it is not, the board would have to look into the hearing provided in order to reach its conclusion as to whether the teacher should be dismissed; for only the board in corporate action can dismiss a teacher. In Chapter IX attention is given to the legal essentials of a school board hearing.

The fourth element is an appeal procedure open to a teacher in the event of dismissal following the hearing. Many tenure laws provide expressly for an appeal and prescribe procedures for it. In any case review by courts would be generally available on a substantial allegation by the teacher that facts alleged had not been proved, that facts proved did not constitute grounds for dismissal, that procedures mandated by the statute were not observed, or that "due process" was not afforded the teacher.

Changing Employment Conditions. The power of a local board to establish conditions of employment within statutory limits for new teachers in a school system is well established. Changes affecting those already employed can be made by state legislatures or local boards provided no contract rights are infringed. This rule often is not easy to apply. In fact the United States Supreme Court decided two cases on the point in consecutive years, holding in 1937 that the New Jersey tenure law did not create a contractual obligation and in 1938 that the Indiana law did.

The New Jersey case involved the reduction of salary of all employees in a local district under authority of a permissive statute enacted in 1933 when economic conditions were depressed. Some teachers contended that this reduction impaired the obligation of their contracts in violation of the United States Constitution. The United States Supreme Court affirmed the holding of the New Jersey courts to the effect that the tenure law created a legislative status for teachers, not a contractual one. The court said:

> Although the . . . [tenure act] prohibited the board, a creature of the state, from reducing the teacher's salary or discharging him without cause, we agree with the courts below that this was but a regulation of the conduct of the board and not a term of a continuing contract of indefinite duration with the individual teacher. . . . [40]

The following year the tenure law of Indiana was held by the United States Supreme Court to have created contractual rights for teachers. This case involved a teacher who had acquired tenure under an act which had subsequently been repealed. When she was not rehired by a local board, she brought suit with the contention that she could not be dismissed without following the tenure procedure. Her claim was sustained by the United States Supreme Court, which, in reversing the holding of the Supreme Court of Indiana, found that the word "contract" had appeared many times in the tenure statute and that earlier decisions in Indiana under the law had construed the statute as creating contract rights. In discussing the issue, the court said:

> The principal function of a legislative body is not to make contracts but to make laws which declare the policy of the state and are subject to repeal when a subsequent Legislature shall determine to alter that policy. Nevertheless, it is established that a legislative enactment may contain provisions which, when accepted as the basis of action by individuals, become contracts between them and the State or its subdivisions. . . .

> Our decisions recognize that every contract is made subject to the implied condition that its fulfillment may be frustrated by a proper exercise of the police power but we have repeatedly said that, in order to have this effect, the exercise of the power must be for an end which is in fact public and the means adopted must be reasonably adapted to that end. . . . [41]

Thus the language of the statute and the desirability or necessity of change for purposes of public policy are pivotal points in determining whether an employment condition for an already employed teacher may be subsequently changed. It is pertinent to note, however, that in a great majority of the cases tenure laws have been held to be amendable.

Causes for Dismissal

Many of the numerous cases pertaining to discharge of teachers involve narrow fact situations or fine points of law in particular jurisdictions. There are, however, some generalizations regarding causes for dismissal which can be illustrated by representative cases.

It is pertinent to note here that there is a legal presumption of competence on the part of a duly certificated teacher. Generally the longer the teacher has held his certificate the stronger is the presumption.

Also in favor of a teacher against whom charges are made is the length of time he has served the system, for it is reasoned that if he had not been competent during his prior service he would have been removed earlier. Proving incompetence is made difficult for some administrators and boards because frequently records specific enough to constitute evidence in court have not been kept.

The situation is further complicated by the indefiniteness of the term incompetence. In one case the Supreme Court of Pennsylvania held that a teacher could be dismissed for incompetence when she served as a waitress in her husband's beer garden, occasionally drank beer with customers in the presence of pupils, and occasionally shook dice for drinks. The court found that such conduct caused her to lose the respect which was necessary for carrying on her work as a teacher.[42]

Other extensions of incompetence beyond inability to perform at a satisfactory level of technical proficiency have been permitted by courts. In Florida in 1944, dismissal of a conscientious objector to war on the ground of incompetence was upheld by the highest court of that state. A statute required teachers "to embrace every opportunity to inculcate, by precept and example, the principles of . . . patriotism. . . ." The court said:

> The Statute . . . imposed the duty to teach the students . . . by precept and example "honesty and patriotism," and the true test of patriotism can accurately be measured by the willingness of the citizen to bear arms and fight in the defense of his Country. The [teacher's] qualifications . . . failed to conform with the requirements of our law. . . . [43]

Inclusion of physical disability under incompetence has been upheld. The Supreme Court of Pennsylvania in 1943 went so far as to sustain a dismissal on the ground of incompetence in the case of a pregnant teacher. The court's opinion included the following:

> We must bear in mind that . . . [the teacher] was not being discriminated against because of her marriage. . . . Her dismissal was due neither to that fact nor to her legitimate pregnancy, but because she became incompetent due to her physical incapacity to discharge her duties.[44]

Immorality, often specifically listed as a cause for dismissal but also recognized under the common law as a basis for disqualification, has been held "not essentially confined to a deviation from sex morality; it may be such a course of conduct as offends the morals of the community and is a bad example to the youth whose ideals a teacher is supposed to foster and to elevate."[45] Thus gambling, drinking, fighting, and acts of misconduct involving arrests or fines or extensive newspaper publicity have been upheld by courts as legal bases for dismissal of teachers.

"Conduct unbecoming a teacher" and "unprofessional conduct" are other omnibus charges upon proof of which teachers may be discharged. In each case involving such charges, the court must decide whether the facts proved by the board actually constitute proscribed conduct. There are several cases related to teacher loyalty where statements and actions of teachers have been held to constitute unprofessional conduct within the tenure statutes. An example is a case where the court approved the dismissal of a history teacher who made "un-American statements in her classroom derogatory to the United States government" and who wrote a letter of congratulation to a former student who failed to register for the draft.[46]

Issues related to reductions of number of teachers in a system frequently are litigated. Laws on this point vary from those outlining a detailed procedure in determining seniority to those not mentioning it at all. Clearly a justifiable decrease in number of teaching positions would constitute grounds for dismissal, since tenure is not designed to force the retention of teachers when there is no work for them to do. This problem has been accentuated by the recent emphasis on consolidation of school districts.

It is rather well settled that, in the absence of a statute to the contrary, a teacher who has acquired tenure rights may not be dismissed if there are in the system other positions for which he is qualified held by those without tenure or those with a shorter period under tenure than his. In the words of one court, in ordering a teacher reinstated:

> Absent grounds personal to the teacher, to terminate her services it was necessary to show affirmatively that there was no position available in which she was qualified to teach.[47]

Another court has discussed the issue as follows:

> Seniority is a matter not to be treated lightly. . . . A schoolboard has not done its duty simply because it has retained no one with less continuous years teaching the subject which the suspended teacher was qualified to

teach. Where a reduction in teaching staff is called for, the Board's first consideration should be how to retain those teachers with the longest years of service by realigning the staff so that the remaining teachers, after the reduction has been effected, can teach the subjects of those who, because of lesser seniority rights, have been suspended.[48]

In connection with abolishing positions, consideration is given by courts to the good faith of the action. A New Jersey case, for example, involved the abolition by a school board of the position of principal, a position covered by the tenure law, and the creation of one called teaching principal and not under the law. The board removed the principal but then assigned his former duties to the new teaching principal. In invalidating this rather apparent subterfuge, the court indicated that it looked to "the substance rather than the form."[49]

A recent case before the Supreme Court of Washington concerned the dismissal of a principal for "gross insubordination and unprofessional conduct." The principal had been attacked in public by the board and in an editorial of a newspaper published by a board member. The principal then somewhat intemperately criticized the board and was discharged. The court ruled that, in the circumstances, the principal had been illegally discharged. It held that he had been so provoked by the board that his intemperate language was not ground for removal. In the words of the court:

> Teachers are required to exercise a high degree of patience and self-control when dealing with their youthful charges; but in their relations with adults, including school board members, they should be judged by the ordinary standards of civility applicable to the particular relationship. If sufficiently provoked, any person may momentarily lose his self-control, and his conduct must be judged accordingly.[50]

LOYALTY

The period following World War II has been marked by the enactment of a great body of legislation related to subversive activities of public school personnel. As might be expected from both the quantity of legislation and the nature of its purpose, copious litigation has resulted. Almost all of it has focused on the methods adopted on state and local levels to assure that there are no disloyal teachers in the public schools. It seems beyond question that proved subversives can be removed from such employment.

The most common approach to the problem of teacher loyalty has been through state laws prescribing oaths. In many areas, local boards have instituted their own loyalty oath requirements regardless of whether a state oath law existed. Some boards have required that certain questions about teachers' activities and associations be answered under oath.

Regarding the constitutionality of an oath requirement as a condition for employment as a teacher, the many courts that have ruled on the point are in agreement that a loyalty oath may be prescribed in the absence of some special state constitutional bar. The Supreme Court of New Jersey in upholding that state's oath requirement for teachers stated the reasoning as follows:

> The aim is not to stifle beliefs as such, but to disqualify for teaching one who, however capacitated otherwise, believes in the objective of overthrow of the government, Federal or state, by force or violence or other unlawful means. . . . One so mentally conditioned is deemed unsuited for the instruction of youth in the schools supported by public funds.[51]

When the board of education of Cleveland instituted an oath requirement, its action was challenged by a taxpayer. The board resolution requested present employees and required prospective employees to sign oaths of nonmembership in the Communist Party or in organizations advocating violent overthrow of the government. The court held that the requirement was within the discretion of the board. In the language of the court:

> It is obvious . . . that we cannot conclude that the members of defendant board illegally expended any of its money, exceeded its powers as a state board, nor deprived its employees of any rights constitutional nor otherwise.[52]

Although it is well settled that a loyalty oath may be required of public school employees, the content of an oath may render it judicially unacceptable. The United States Supreme Court in 1952 declared an Oklahoma oath law unconstitutional because of the provisions contained in the oath. The primary basis for invalidating the law was the fact that disqualification was based on membership during the preceding five years in an organization determined to be subversive, regardless of whether or not the person involved knew of the character of the organization at the time of membership. The court spoke as follows:

> But membership may be innocent. A state servant may have joined a proscribed organization unaware of its activities and purposes. In recent years, many completely loyal persons have severed organizational ties after learning for the first time of the character of groups to which they had belonged. . . . Yet under the Oklahoma Act, the fact of association alone determines disloyalty and disqualification; it matters not whether association existed innocently or knowingly. . . . . Indiscriminate classification of innocent with knowing activity must fall as an assertion of arbitrary power. The oath offends due process.[53]

The United States Supreme Court has upheld the constitutionality of the widely publicized Feinberg Anti-Subversive Law in New York. This statute, without prescribing an oath, makes membership in a subversive organization prima facie evidence of disqualification for appointment or retention in the public schools of the state and requires local boards to file annual reports on the loyalty of teachers. In its opinion sustaining this law, the Supreme Court said:

> If, under the procedure set up in the New York law, a person is found to be unfit and is disqualified from employment in the public school system because of membership in a listed organization, he is not thereby denied the right of free speech and assembly. His freedom of choice between membership in the organization and employment in the school system might be limited, but not his freedom of speech or assembly, except in the remote sense that limitation is inherent in every choice. Certainly such limitation is not one the state may not make in the exercise of its police power to protect the schools from pollution and thereby to defend its existence.

The court went on to state that "one's associates, past and present, as well as one's conduct may properly be considered in determining fitness and loyalty." Three of the Justices dissented in this case.[54]

In 1956 the United States Supreme Court by a five-to-four majority held unconstitutional a provision in the New York City Charter which provided for the automatic termination of employment of any employee who refused to answer questions regarding his official conduct put by a duly authorized body. The case arose when a teacher at a publicly supported college refused to testify before a Congressional committee investigating Communist activities. The opinion included the following:

This is not to say that Slochower has a constitutional right to be an associate professor of German at Brooklyn College. The State has broad powers in the selection and discharge of its employees, and it may be that proper inquiry would show Slochower's continued employment to be inconsistent with a real interest in the State. But there has been no such inquiry here. We hold that the summary dismissal of appellant violates due process of law.[55]

CITATIONS

1. Johnson v. School District No. 14, 70 Wyo. 407, 250 P.2d 890 (1952).
2. People *ex rel.* Fursman v. Chicago, 278 Ill. 218, 116 N.E. 158 (1917).
3. Hutton v. Gill, 212 Ind. 164, 8 N.E.2d 818 (1937).
4. Fry v. Board of Education, 17 Cal.2d 753, 112 P. 2d 229 (1941).
5. Frisk v. Board of Education of Duluth, 246 Minn. 366, 75 N.W.2d 504 (1956).
6. Alston v. School Board of Norfolk, 112 F.2d 992 (C.C.A. 4th, Virginia, 1940).
7. Aebli v. Board of Education, 62 Cal. App.2d 706, 145 P.2d 601 (1944).
8. Rible v. Hughes, 24 Cal.2d 437, 150 P.2d 455 (1944).
9. Kacsur v. Board of Trustees, 18 Cal.2d 586, 116 P.2d 593 (1941).
10. Heinlein v. Anaheim Union High School District, 96 Cal. App.2d 19, 214 P.2d 536 (1950).
11. Murphy v. School Committee of Lawrence, 321 Mass. 478, 73 N.E.2d 835 (1947).
12. Appeal of Ritzie, 372 Pa. 588, 94 A.2d 729 (1953).
13. Dugas v. Ascension Parish School Board, 81 So.2d 817 (La. 1955).
14. Bacon v. Board of Education of City of New York, 122 N.Y.S.2d 98 (1953).
15. Parrish v. Moss, 106 N.Y.S.2d 577 (1951).
16. Cotter v. City of Chelsea, 329 Mass. 314, 108 N.E.2d 47 (1952).
17. Hutton v. Gill, *supra* note 3.
18. Liva v. Board of Education, 126 N.J.L. 221, 18 A.2d 704 (1941).
19. Offhouse v. State Board of Education, 131 N.J.L. 391, 36 A.2d 884 (1944).
20. Phelps v. Board of Education of West New York, 300 U.S. 319, 57 S.Ct. 483 (1937).
21. McMinn County Board of Education v. Anderson, 292 S.W.2d 198 (Tenn. 1956).
22. State v. Davidson County, 198 Tenn. 24, 277 S.W.2d 396 (1954).

23. Talbott v. Independent School District, 230 Ia. 949, 299 N.W. 556 (1941).
24. Nelson v. Board of Directors, 246 Ia. 1079, 70 N.W.2d 555 (1955).
25. Birnbaum v. New York State Teachers Retirement System, 150 N.Y.S.2d 620 (1956).
26. Newcomb v. Ogden City Public School Teachers' Retirement Commission, 121 Utah 503, 243 P.2d 941 (1952).
27. State *ex rel.* Holton v. City of Tampa, 118 Fl. 370, 159 So. 292 (1934).
28. Dodge v. Board of Education, 302 U.S. 74, 58 S. Ct. 98 (1937).
29. Clarke v. Ireland, 122 Mont. 191, 199 P.2d 965 (1948).
30. State *ex rel.* Holmes v. Krueger, 271 Wis. 129, 72 N.W.2d 734 (1955).
31. Averell v. City of Newburyport, 241 Mass. 333, 135 N.E. 463 (1922).
32. Loomis v. Board of Education of Philadelphia, 376 Pa. 428, 103 A.2d 769 (1954).
33. School City of East Chicago v. Sigler, 219 Ind. 9, 36 N.E.2d 760 (1941).
34. City of Manchester v. Manchester Teachers Guild, 131 A.2d 59 (N. H. 1957).
35. Norwalk Teachers' Association v. Board of Education, 138 Conn. 269, 83 A.2d 482 (1951).
36. Fowler v. Town of Enfield, 138 Conn. 521, 86 A.2d 662 (1952).
37. Board of Education v. Public School Employees Union, 233 Minn. 144, 45 N.W.2d 797 (1951).
38. Norwalk Teachers' Association v. Board of Education, *supra* note 35.
39. Crawfordsville v. Hays, 42 Ind. 200 (1873).
40. Phelps v. Board of Education of West New York, *supra* note 20.
41. Indiana *ex rel.* Anderson v. Brand, 303 U.S. 95, 58 S. Ct. 43 (1938).
42. Horosko v. Mt. Pleasant Township School District, 335 Pa. 369, 6 A.2d 866 (1939).
43. State *ex rel.* Schweitzer v. Turner, 155 Fl. 270, 19 So.2d 832 (1944).
44. Appeal of School District of Bethlehem, 347 Pa. 418, 32 A.2d 565 (1943).
45. Horosko v. Mt. Pleasant Township School District, *supra* note 42.
46. Joyce v. Board of Education of City of Chicago, 325 Ill. App. 543, 60 N.E.2d 431 (1945).
47. Swisher v. Darden, 59 N.M. 511, 287 P.2d 73 (1955).
48. Welsko v. Foster Township School District, 383 Pa. 390, 119 A.2d 43 (1956).
49. Viemeister v. Board of Education, 5 N.J.Super. 215, 68 A.2d 768 (1949).

50. Appeal of Coates, 287 P.2d 102 (Wash. 1955).
51. Thorp v. Board of Trustees, 6 N.J. 498, 79 A.2d 462 (1951).
52. Dworken v. Cleveland Board of Education, 108 N.E.2d 103 (Ohio 1951).
53. Wieman v. Updegraff, 344 U.S. 183, 73 S.Ct. 215 (1952).
54. Adler v. Board of Education of City of New York, 342 U.S. 485, 72 S.Ct. 380 (1952).
55. Slochower v. Board of Higher Education of City of New York, 350 U.S. 551, 76 S.Ct. 637 (1956).

V

THE AUTHORITY OF SCHOOL BOARDS IN RELATION TO SCHOOL PROPERTY

IN GENERAL

All school buildings are deemed the property of the state, as distinguished from the school district or the local municipality. Statutes usually vest the titles in the local district or in the board as trustees for the public at large. School boards generally are responsible for maintenance and repair of buildings, although in some areas municipalities have been given this function by statute. "Repair" must be distinguished from "improving" or "remodeling." The latter normally requires special approval of the electorate; the former is an implied power, if not an express one, arising from the responsibility for operating the schools. "Repair" is taken to mean "restore to a sound or good state after decay, injury, dilapidation, or partial destruction." [1]

Determination of school building uses is completely in the power of the state legislature, except for possible constitutional restrictions. A number of states have enacted legislation which in varying degrees authorizes local boards to exercise discretion in the use of school buildings for other than school purposes. Other states have neither spelled out legitimate uses of school buildings nor expressly granted authority to determine uses to local boards. In the latter situation the cases are not in agreement; that is, in some states courts will not permit wide use without statutory authority, whereas in others the reverse has been true. Through the years many states by legislative enactments have broadened the uses to which school buildings may be put, and a tendency of the courts to become more liberal in this regard with the passage of time can be noted.

76

There are two basic general legal objections which have been raised against local boards' permitting the use of school buildings for non-school purposes. The more important one goes back to the fundamental concept that boards of education are agencies of limited powers and their authority does not extend to areas into which the legislature has not expressly permitted them to operate. The second, more often raised in older cases, is that a non-school use constitutes an expenditure of public tax money for private purposes and therefore is illegal. Charging of fees to cover expenses or for profit does not reduce the weight of these two arguments according to some courts.

There are other objections applied to special groups or special purposes. Problems of church–state relations enter in the use of property by religious groups, and issues of partisan politics as well as of subversive activities appear in relation to civic groups or groups alleged to be supporting particular political points of view. Owners of business establishments may object to use of school property for non-school activities in possible competition with their businesses. Some may feel that the schools should be confined to teaching the "three R's" and that therefore certain types of "extracurricular" activities should not be held in school buildings for pupils, much less for citizens at large.

It is interesting to note that this attitude supporting limited use of school property is essentially one which emphasizes historically an older philosophy of the role of public education. Yet, almost exactly the opposing point of view also is deep-rooted in our history. In the smaller communities of the country, particularly on the frontier, it was not unusual to find school-houses used for all sorts of social and civic activities simply because there were often no other suitable buildings. Thus, historical public policy is hard to assess in the nation as a whole. Courts across the nation certainly have not been consistent. It is true that the statutory situation has varied, but the same types of statutes have been construed differently by different courts. Changing community attitudes and concepts of sound public policy as well as new legislation have persuaded courts within several states to alter their stands with the passage of time in favor of wider permissible use. In the words of one court:

> Boards of education, supported by public sentiment and interest, now commit school districts to various measures and activities which our

fathers would have regarded as revolutionary and intolerable. Measures which were once discarded, if they were ever considered in educational affairs, are demonstrably efficient in advancing the interests of education generally.[2]

COMMUNITY USES IN GENERAL

It is well established that the holding of school-connected activities to which parents and friends are invited are legally justifiable. This has been held true even if fees are charged and the general public is urged to attend through advertising techniques.[3] Application has been made to instances where the student body sponsored lectures, dances, motion picture shows, musical shows, athletics, and the like.

In a broad and widely cited interpretation of a typical general statute, the Supreme Court of Wyoming stated the general rule as follows:

> So long as the proper maintenance and conduct of the school is not interfered with, or in any wise hampered, and so long as school district property is neither injured, defaced, nor destroyed, as we view it, our law vests a generous amount of discretion in the school district electors, in regular meeting assembled, concerning what use shall be made of the school district property when it is not in actual service for formal school sessions. Our Legislatures, over a period of some sixty years, have thought is quite safe, evidently, to trust such matters to the sound judgment of the several communities of the state in determining their respective needs. That this is a wise and salutary arrangement we have not the slightest doubt. It is especially manifest in view of the broadening sphere of educational activities. With that discretion we must decline to interfere in the case at bar, for in our judgment the law defining the powers of school districts has not been transgressed.

In this case the owner of a hall which was rented for dances and other social events brought suit to prevent the use of a new school building for other than school purposes. The school building was being used for social gatherings, and no charge was being made by the school board.[4]

The two criteria—no interference with the school program and no damage to the school building—are always basic. In some situations they are the only standards advanced as tests of whether school boards have exceeded their powers in permitting community groups to use school facilities. A concise statement of this legal philosophy regarding the role of schools has been made by the Supreme Court of Rhode Island in an old case where it was said:

> Our school system, with all the intellectual and material means for instruction provided by it, was designed to promote public education; and any use of the school property tending to this end, and which does not interfere with the regular schools, may be permitted by the trustees of a school district, as within the spirit of their trust.

Upheld in that case was the use of the school building after hours for private instruction in vocal music.[5]

Whether fees to cover expenses of light, heat, and custodial service are required of community groups using facilities for social and recreational purposes apparently has not been a crucial factor in judicial decisions as to whether such use is permissible.

Relatively rarely does a statute remove discretion from local boards and require them to open their buildings for non-school use. California has perhaps gone further in this regard than any other state and has a statute which has led to much litigation. Essentially it provides that local boards must grant free use of school facilities to

> . . . citizens, parent-teachers' association, Campfire Girls, Boy Scout troops, farmers' organizations, clubs, and associations formed for recreational, educational, political, economic, artistic, or moral activities of the public school districts . . . [for purposes of] supervised recreational activities . . . [and discussions of] any subjects and questions which in their [the group's] judgment appertain to the educational, political, economic, artistic and moral interests of the citizens of the communities.

The local board may adopt "reasonable rules and regulations" to carry out the above and in no case can such use interfere with the regular purposes of the schools.

Under this statute, a local board has been upheld in refusing use of school facilities to a group which intended to have as speaker a person who, when previously he had spoken in other communities, had roused so much organized opposition that disturbances had resulted. The board felt that classes in session at that time would be disturbed.[6]

In a New York case a local board had granted permission to a church organization to hold a concert in a school auditorium. Subsequent to the granting of the permission, the board learned that the featured singer

was a man who had been named by a Congressional committee as supporting organizations fronting for the Communist Party. The board was barred
by court action from rescinding the permit, largely because it had no
regulation reserving the right to do so and vested interests had accrued
between the granting of the permit and the attempt to cancel it.[7]

In 1955 the United States Supreme Court accepted its first case
relative to use of school buildings by outside groups. It was a case complicated by technical procedural questions, but the essential facts were that a
board of education in New York had refused to permit a group known as
the Committee for Peace to use the school facilities. The board assigned
no specific reason for the refusal. The Committee claimed its rights were
violated by alleged discrimination against it when "organizations of a
similar character" had been granted use. The Committee failed to name
any such organizations. The New York courts did not pass on the merits
of the case, but quoted with approval from another opinion as follows:

> "Schools are established and maintained for a definite and specific pur-
> pose, to wit, the secular education of youth of the State, and any activity
> within the scope of that purpose or tending to promote the welfare of
> the schools and the community should be allowed and encouraged. On
> the other hand, any activity which is not embraced in the general school
> program and which is of a controversial nature liable to arouse ill feel-
> ing, jealousy or dissention; or to lead to misunderstanding, should be
> rigidly debarred. . . . The public schools are supported by the whole body
> of citizens; within their walls assemble the children of the rich and the
> poor, the children of parents of every shade of religious belief and un-
> belief. . . . Therefore, nothing that will tend to foster intolerance, bigotry,
> animosity or dissention should be allowed to inject itself into the public
> school system of this great state."[8]

The United States Supreme Court, after hearing arguments, decided by
a five-to-four vote of the Justices that on procedural grounds the case
should be dismissed, thereby in effect leaving the school board determination intact.[9]

In subsequent litigation the same plaintiff cited some organizations
allegedly in the same category as the Committee for Peace which had been
allowed by the board to use school buildings for meetings. The board of
education stated that a previous meeting of the group had caused strife
and dissension in the community where it was held and that the petitioner,
who was in the linoleum business, had put advertisements in Communist

periodicals. The commissioner of education supported the board and a lower court sustained the decision of the commissioner. The appellate court, however, reversed the judgment, primarily on the ground that the lower court had not taken evidence regarding whether other groups similarly situated had been permitted to use school facilities. In its opinion the court stated the following:

> ... school authorities may not deny to one organization the use of school buildings and permit such use to other organizations in the same category, all factors being reasonably equal. This appears to be plain common sense. School authorities may, if they choose, close the door to all outside organizations, but if they open the door they must treat alike all organizations in the same category. . . . A School Board of course is not a censor, and its duty so far as school buildings are concerned is merely to regulate and protect them. We do not take it that it may discriminate against an organization simply because it, or even a part of the public, may be hostile to the opinions or program of such organization provided the same are not unlawful per se. If fair proof is presented that a clear and present danger exists that public disorder and possible damage to the school property will result from a proposed use then we think the Board would be within its discretionary power to deny such a use. Justifiable exclusion is not discrimination.[9a]

POLITICAL USES

The last three cases discussed in the preceding section have political implications. A case squarely involving the use of a school building by a political group arose when a California board was prevented by a court from barring, in a school building, a meeting for discussion of the Socialist Party's position on peace. The court found that the board had granted the use of its building "to sundry associations of citizens organized for political and partisan purposes" and that the board was unable to "prove the subversive nature of the applicant society or organization."[10]

In another case the Supreme Court of California ruled that a board of education could not require of a particular group an oath of non-advocacy of subversive doctrines or of non-membership in groups so advocating as a condition precedent to the use of school facilities. In invalidating a state law aimed at barring subversives from use of buildings, the court said:

The state is under no duty to make school buildings available for public meetings. . . . If it elects to do so, however, it cannot arbitrarily prevent any members of the public from holding such meetings. . . . Nor can it make the privilege of holding them dependent on conditions that would deprive any members of the public of their constitutional rights. A state is without power to impose an unconstitutional requirement as a condition for granting a privilege even though the privilege is the use of state property. . . . Since the state cannot compel "subversive elements" directly to renounce their convictions and affiliations, it cannot make such a renunciation a condition of receiving the privilege of free assembly in a school building.[11]

RELIGIOUS USES

Religious meetings designed to give instruction in or to propagate a particular religious faith generally are not permissible in public school buildings, mainly because of state constitutional provisions regarding church and state relationships. There are, however, exceptions. Many courts have drawn a distinction between religious services and educational or cultural activities sponsored by the members of a particular denomination. One court has stated the rule concisely as follows:

It is the use to which the school buildings are put, and not the identity of the users, that is decisive of the lawfulness of the use.[12]

Also involved is the issue of short-term or long-term use. There are numerous older decisions sustaining the temporary use of school facilities for religious purposes.[13]

It seems settled that a local board may bar all activities with religious connotations if it so desires. In a 1950 case, a board of education refused members of Jehovah's Witnesses the use of a high school auditorium for a series of Bible lectures. The rule of the board ("permits shall not be granted to anyone for any religious or sectarian purpose") was sustained by the Supreme Court of Pennsylvania. The court said:

Whether the school property shall be used by any group at all is a matter resting within the discretion of each board of school directors. This court is not a superboard of school directors in performance of an official duty. The legislature has delegated this power to the school boards, not to the courts. In the absence of any proof of unreasonableness or an arbitrary or capricious exercise of the power, the judgment of the board must stand.[14]

Another case involving Jehovah's Witnesses occurred in 1949 in Ohio. There the board had refused the group permission to use facilities although a statute provided that local boards upon payment of a reasonable fee, should make buildings available for educational, religious, and other meetings and "for such other purposes as may make for the welfare of the community." The court upheld the board on the basis that the board had fairly determined that such use would not "make for the welfare of the community" because of the resentment against granting permission which was present in the town.[15]

RENTING SCHOOL FACILITIES

The states vary in their legal attitudes toward the renting or leasing of school property. That school property was intended for school use only, or at the limit, for community use, is one basis for holding that school boards have no such power in the absence of a statute granting it. Another is that the renting of facilities would give the school board a character alien to its prime purpose. Also, competition with private commercial enterprises is involved.

The charging of fees to cover actual expenses incurred in use of the building by non-school groups is not considered renting, and, in the absence of a statute to the contrary, is generally permissible. On the other hand it is not normally required that boards charge rental fees for such use. If there is a statute providing that use shall be free to certain groups, a court has held that a board may not, as a condition on which permission depends, require the users to furnish a public liability insurance policy to protect the district against damage claims for injuries suffered by those attending the non-school meeting. This would constitute a charge and be prohibited under the statute.[16]

Where renting has been judicially approved the courts note that the twin criteria of no interference with the school program and no damage to the building are observed. Also the character of the renters and the use made by renters are considered. Use by fraternal orders for meetings and use for providing recreational activities and public entertainment have been frequently sustained.[17] In other cases, however, rentals have been strictly barred by courts in similar circumstances.[18]

Whether school property is used for an event for which there is an admission charge and the purposes of the charge are factors to be considered. So is the ultimate purpose of the activity. If the use is essentially in the public interest or for a community purpose, even though incidental private gain is involved, it is likely to be sustained, according to the weight of authority. In regard to the question, Can public school facilities be used for conducting studies or classes for which tuition is charged and paid to the person or persons giving the instruction?, different courts have given different answers.[19]

Renting of property raises some important questions of liability, which are discussed in Chapter X. Insurance protection and governmental immunity from certain liabilities may not cover circumstances arising from rental of school facilities.

There are conflicting decisions as to whether school land can be leased for continuing commercial purposes. For example, when oil has been discovered on school property, some state courts have approved the granting of leases, while others have not.[20]

School property cannot be sold, however, except in strict compliance with applicable statutes. Neither can it be given away by a school board regardless of the worthiness of the purpose to which it might be put. The reasoning developed by an Arizona court is pertinent. There, where the community needed a hospital, the school district leased one of its buildings to the hospital commission for that purpose for one dollar a year, the commission having an option to renew. The court in invalidating the arrangement reasoned:

> School districts are created by the state for the sole purpose of promoting the education of the youth of the state. All their powers are given them and all the property which they own is held by them in trust for the same purpose, and any contract . . . which . . . is not meant for the educational advancement of the youth of the district but for some other purpose, no matter how worthy in nature, is ultra vires and void.[21]

USES CONFLICTING WITH PRIVATE BUSINESSES

Many uses of school property may be alleged to conflict with legitimate private interests. Cases involving selling of food and school supplies, furnishing halls for plays and dances, making available gymnasiums and stadiums for athletic contests, and the like have been common. Obviously, some of the uses previously noted as having been judicially approved in some jurisdictions could interfere with private businesses. If the school-endorsed activity is primarily for commercial gain, generally it will be enjoined by a court on petition of an aggrieved businessman. There is a vast twilight zone, however, where school or community purposes are served at the same time that some private individual's business might suffer. The more desirable the public purpose served, the more likely are the courts to sustain the use of school facilities.

It is apparent that the operation of a cafeteria by a school could decrease the volume of business of a lunchroom proprietor. Yet such activity has uniformly been sustained by courts where the object could be held to be primarily the benefit of pupils (convenience, balanced diets, discipline) and not profit. This basic purpose has been held not to be subverted by selling meals to teachers, employees, and an occasional parent.[22] Furthermore, a school board may require children to eat in the school cafeteria if they do not bring their lunches or go home to eat. It may not, however, set up an activity or regulation designed deliberately to destroy some business establishment. If legal malice can be proved, the board would be enjoined from sponsoring the activity or enforcing the rule.

In general, provisions in schools for selling supplies to students at cost, have been upheld by courts, although there is some authority to the contrary.[23] If a profit is involved, particularly if it is more than incidental and if the proceeds do not go directly into a school fund, such sale probably would be prohibited. Essentially the same general considerations apply here as in the cafeteria and the rental of facilities situations.

CITATIONS

1. *Black's Law Dictionary,* Fourth Edition, Page 1462.
2. Kuhn v. Board of Education of Detroit, 175 Mich. 438, 141 N.W. 574 (1913).
3. Beard v. Board of Education, 81 Utah 51, 16 P.2d 900 (1932).
4. Merryman v. School District No. 16, 43 Wyo. 376, 5 P.2d 267 (1931).
5. Appeal of Barnes, 6 R.I. 591 (1860).

6. Payroll Guarantee Association v. Board of Education, 27 Cal.2d 197, 163 P.2d 433 (1945).
7. Cannon v. Towner, 188 Misc. 955, 70 N.Y.S.2d 303 (1947).
8. Ellis v. Dixon, 118 N.Y.S.2d 815 (1953).
9. Ellis v. Dixon, 349 U. S. 458, 75 S.Ct. 850 (1955).
9a. Ellis v. Allen, 4 App. Div.2d 343, 165 N.Y.S.2d 624 (1957).
10. Goodman v. Board of Education, 48 Cal. App.2d 731, 120 P.2d 665 (1941).
11. Danskin v. San Diego Unified School District, 28 Cal.2d 536, 171 P.2d 885 (1946).
12. Lewis v. Board of Education, 157 Misc. 520, 285 N.Y.S. 164 (1935).
13. Nichols v. School Directors, 93 Ill. 61 (1879).
14. McKnight v. Board of Public Education, 365 Pa. 422, 76 A.2d 207 (1950).
15. State v. Grand Rapids Board of Education, 88 Ohio App. 364, 100 N.E.2d 294 (1949).
16. Ellis v. Board of Education, 27 Cal.2d 322, 164 P.2d 1 (1945).
17. Young v. Broadwater County High School, 90 Mont. 576, 4 P.2d 725 (1931).
18. Sugar v. Monroe, 108 La. 677, 32 So. 961 (1902).
19. Cf. Weir v. Day, 35 Ohio St. 143 (1878) and Appeal of Barnes, *supra* note 5.
20. Cf. Herald v. Board of Education, 65 W.Va. 765, 65 S.E. 102 (1909), and Williams v. McKenzie, 203 Ky. 376, 262 S.W. 598 (1924).
21. Prescott Community Hospital Commission v. Prescott School District, 57 Ariz. 492, 115 P.2d 160 (1941).
22. Goodman v. School District No. 1, 32 F.2d 586 (1929).
23. Cf. Cook v. Chamberlain, 199 Wis. 42, 225 N.W. 141 (1929), and Kuhn v. Board of Education of Detroit, *supra* note 2.

VI

THE AUTHORITY OF SCHOOL BOARDS
IN RELATION TO SCHOOL FUNDS

IN GENERAL

School funds essentially are of two kinds: general and special. General funds, those which may be used for any nonprohibited school purpose, constitute most of the funds referred to in this section. Special funds are those authorized or allocated for a specified purpose. Special funds may be used only for the purpose stated, and therefore are not so often the subject of litigation as are general funds. However, whether a particular expenditure item falls within a specific purpose is often the basis of legal action.

Another broad dual classification of the funds available to local boards is based on how the funds were raised, that is, by taxation or by bond issues. Tax money usually may be used for general school purposes, though there are exceptions. Money raised by bond issues, on the other hand, is almost always for a specific purpose. Another, but for this section less important, broad breakdown of funds is by source: local, county, state, or federal.

There is some inconsistency among the states as to what constitutes a "school purpose" for which funds can legally be spent. Also, chronological differences are noticeable, with more recent judicial holdings more likely to support expenditures in areas removed from the traditional curriculum of the early public schools.

Attention is given in Chapter III to the legal aspects of broadening the curriculum. Since most curricular extensions involve some expenditure of money, many of the cases referred to there arose when taxpayers challenged the expenditure of school monies for them. It was pointed out that the establishment of high schools, kindergartens, and courses in various subjects has been rather uniformly upheld by courts when challenged by taxpayers. Expenditures for health programs within bounds have been sustained. So has the building of gymnasiums and stadiums for athletic contests. Also it has been noted that the operation of cafeterias under certain conditions is a legitimate use of school funds.

USE FOR SUPPLIES AND EQUIPMENT

Supplies and equipment essential to the effective operation of the schools may be purchased by local boards. Other items may not be purchased in the absence of statutes so permitting. The line between these two categories, however, cannot be drawn clearly, and frequently the courts must resolve controversies.

What constitutes necessary equipment has been the subject of several judicial opinions. Generally, and increasingly in more recent times, the courts have tended to sustain the judgment of local boards on this question when the statutes do not prohibit the expenditure and it does not appear frivolous. In the words of the Supreme Court of Oklahoma:

> . . . the Legislature did not intend to so restrict such Board as to limit expenses only for things indispensable to the maintenance and operation of its public school system; and we conclude that such expenses as are convenient, useful, appropriate, suitable, proper or conducive to the desired ends of the general program, and to the conduct of such school system, are authorized to be incurred thereunder in the discretion of the Board, unless otherwise restricted by law.

In this case the purchase of school band uniforms was upheld where the board deemed it necessary to the "needs of the pupils who are receiving instructions in band music."[1]

This criterion of close relationship between the equipment and instruction is a pivotal one so far as authorized expenditures of funds are concerned. Several courts have advanced as another criterion the proportion of the student body receiving the benefit of the supplies. This consideration has appeared in situations involving expensive equipment used only by the members of a team in competitive athletics.

In connection with health programs, it has been pointed out that doctors, dentists, and nurses may be employed for examination and diagnostic purposes. However, the purchase of sleeping garments to be worn for extra warmth in open air classes by pupils susceptible to tuberculosis has been held not to be within the implied powers of a local board.[2]

Most states now have statutes pertaining to free textbooks and to the ways of financing them. Actually, there are several old holdings by courts that the power to furnish free textbooks is not an implied power of local boards and that they cannot furnish texts unless specifically authorized by statute.[3] The question of the right of the state to furnish free texts has been answered by courts in the affirmative from the beginning.

The United States Supreme Court has sustained the right of a state to distribute the same books on the same basis to children in non-public schools as are furnished children in public schools. This case, decided in 1930, is the basis of the "child benefit" doctrine which distinguishes in theory between use of public funds for the benefit of the individual child in the public interest and use of public funds for the benefit of private interests. The former is legally permissible whereas the latter is not. In the case in point, the United States Supreme Court quoted with approval from the opinion of the Supreme Court of Louisiana as follows:

> The schools, however, are not the beneficiaries of these appropriations [to furnish free texts to all children regardless of school attended]. They obtain nothing from them, nor are they relieved of a single obligation, because of them. The school children and the state alone are the beneficiaries[4]

The distinction drawn by the court is not easy to apply. It should be observed that the church–state issue was not directly raised in this case. Extensions of the "child benefit" doctrine, however, have been advocated to a large extent by parochial school interests and resisted most by those opposed to use of public funds for purposes helpful to sectarian interests.

USE FOR TRANSPORTATION

The prevailing judicial attitude through the years has been not to consider provision of transportation an implied power of boards of education. In the absence of express legislative authority most courts have not permitted boards to transport children. Apparently it was felt that the responsibility for getting children to school lay with the parent and, perhaps, that the exercise of walking was beneficial for children. On the other hand, the constitutionality of state legislation, either mandatory or permissive, in this area has been sustained except in some cases involving conflicts with state constitutions when transportation of pupils to private or sectarian schools was required or permitted. In 1947 by a five-to-four majority the United States Supreme Court found the Federal Constitution to be no bar to a state which wished to furnish such transportation. In this "New Jersey Bus Case" the United States Supreme Court was asked to rule on the constitutionality of a statute authorizing local boards to furnish transportation to all children except those attending private schools operated for profit. It should be emphasized that the holding in this decision is that states *may* provide transportation at public expense to non-public schools; it is *not* that they *must*.[5] In other words, the matter is left to the determination of each state.

Some states, by constitutional provision or by statute, prohibit the use of public funds to transport children to non-public schools. Prohibitions may be based on the issue of use of public funds for private purposes or on that of aid to sectarian groups. Two years after the New Jersey case, the Supreme Court of Washington interpreted the constitution of that state as barring expenditures of public funds to pay for transportation to sectarian schools.[6] Other states specifically permit local districts to furnish such transportation on a local option basis. A few states require that transportation be afforded all children regardless of the non-profit school attended. In still other states, there is no legislation on the subject and judicial decisions have not clarified the issue.

State laws regarding transportation of children may be permissive, mandatory, or a combination specifying some things which must be done and authorizing others. Often a distance from school beyond which transportation must be furnished to children is specified. Usually these laws provide for state aid in paying for such transportation. In most states, local boards may provide for transportation for lesser distances at local expense. Normally the district has the option of operating its own buses, contracting for bus service, reimbursing parents for expenses on public transportation facilities, or sometimes of reimbursing parents who furnish transportation for their own children. Transportation does not have to be door-to-door, but within the limits of distance stated in the pertinent statute.

Generally courts have refused to read into statutes providing for transportation "to and from school" an implied power to furnish such for "extracurricular" activities where attendance is not compulsory. The issue involves authority to use school funds, not whether such activities are beneficial to students. In the words of the Supreme Court of Utah:

> Let it be assumed that ... contests, games and social entertainments, lectures and dramas have a proper place in the educational system, yet the question remains whether the board of education has authority to furnish transportation ... for the purpose of attending such activities. The language of the statute is "transportation to and from school." ... The expenditure of school funds for this purpose was properly enjoined.[7]

USE FOR INSURANCE

Many states specifically authorize the purchase of school building insurance, but in any event the express power to manage and control school property clearly implies the power to purchase insurance for the protection of that property. Details of the insurance program generally are left in the hands of the board. As one court has reasoned:

> In the light of the character of this express power [the power to insure] bestowed upon the board, it is readily apparent that it carries with it all of the implied powers that are reasonably inferential from the express power to accomplish the object for which it was given. It is necessarily implied that the power is bestowed upon the board of education to determine for itself against what casualties it will insure and the amount of risks, the specific buildings and property that it will contract to be insured, the insurance corporation that it will contract with, and the details of the contracts.[8]

There is no such clarity in regard to the purchase of liability insurance. Problems related to liability are discussed in Chapter X. Some courts have held that in a state where school districts are immune from liability in tort they have no right to spend money for liability insurance. The reasoning is supplied by the highest court of West Virginia:

Because it is a public agency, an arm of the state, a school board is not liable for damages for personal injury, even though such injury may arise from neglect or nonfeasance. . . . Nor can a board of education by the acquisition of indemnity insurance, or otherwise, change its status as a governmental agency. . . . It is therefore asserted on behalf of the plaintiff [the district] that inasmuch as the district board could not have been held liable for damages occasioned by the negligent operation of a school bus, there was nothing against which the policy of indemnification could operate. . . .

A function not expressly authorized can be justified only if it comes within clear and plain implications of the statute. . . . Such implications . . . do not arise . . . here.[9]

Other courts have permitted purchase of such insurance. Their reasoning is based on a conviction that the common law doctrine of governmental immunity is no longer valid in modern times. Because a prime basis of the government immunity doctrine is that no funds are available to pay damages and since insurance coverage would provide funds, they hold that if a school board deems it to be its moral obligation to make redress available to pupils and others harmed due to the fault of the district while at school or on school buses, purchase of liability insurance is a legitimate expenditure of school funds.[10]

Whether, in the absence of a statute, local boards can purchase group life and disability insurance for teachers of the district is not clear in many states. Supporting this expenditure in the only ruling directly on the point by an appellate court, the Supreme Court of New Mexico said:

It is admitted that the securing of group insurance for the teachers enables the board of education to procure a better class of teachers, and prevents frequent changes in the teaching force. This is certainly desirable and conducive to the "proper conduct of the public schools." School funds are now being spent in all the school districts of the state, and in many, if not all of the other states, for purposes and objects unquestionably proper, gauged by our advancing civilization, which a quarter of a century ago would have been considered highly improper. . . .

It is clear that the courts should not interfere with the discretion intrusted to boards of education in this state, unless it plainly appears that there has been a gross abuse of discretion, and that the funds are being spent for purposes and objects which have no relation to the public schools. This cannot be said in this case.[11]

This is in line with the majority view that municipalities may provide insurance for their employees. Probably the reasoning would also apply to Workmen's Compensation where teachers are not specifically excluded.

Statutes are clarifying in many states the powers of local boards of education relative to purchase of insurance of various types.

MISCELLANEOUS USES

In most situations, authority to purchase school sites under certain conditions would probably be considered an implied power under general statutes granting powers to local boards to provide for schools. The authority for acquiring land for school buildings normally would include acquisition of areas for playgrounds adjoining the buildings. Several older decisions indicate that purchase of land for other special uses, such as for instruction in agriculture, would require special statutory authorization. There is divided authority on the recent issue of whether purchase of a camp site for use by school children is an implied power of local boards.[12] Also whether local boards have implied power to build residences for staff personnel has been answered in both ways by different courts.[13]

There are several older judicial opinions prohibiting paying expenses of school board members or employees attending educational conventions in the absence of statutory authority for such expenditures. However, in 1940 the implied power of a board to pay the membership fee in a state school boards association was upheld.[14] The power to make such expenditures increasingly is being granted by legislation.

The line between the responsibilities of school boards and those of municipal agencies often becomes faint in practice. Problems related to safety and welfare of children are particularly hard to classify from the point of view of responsibility. Usually cooperation between the school board and the agencies of general government leads to solutions not involving litigation. In this regard it should be pointed out that expenditures of school boards have been held unauthorized in some situations involving putting in a public street in front of a school, furnishing free lunches to pupils whose parents could not afford them, furnishing transportation because of traffic hazards which were in the province of general government agencies to regulate or remove, and employing legal counsel when such was to be provided by a general government agency.

In connection with the employment of legal counsel, an analysis of the cases indicates that such action is generally regarded as an implied power of local boards if not an express one. Also, most courts have sustained the authority of a board to hire additional attorneys in cases where the municipal corporation counsel or district attorney was by law to afford legal services. In any event, lawyers employed by boards must engage only in activities in the public interest of the district.

There are myriad uses for which school boards may contemplate the expenditure of funds in the absence of controlling statutes. In such situations they must decide whether the expenditure would probably be judicially considered to be for a "school purpose" within the framework of existing laws and judicial interpretations in their respective states.

CITATIONS

1. Kay County Excise Board v. Atchison, T. and S. F. Ry. Co., 185 Okl. 327, 91 P.2d 1087 (1939).
2. Board of Education of Cleveland v. Ferguson, 39 NE.2d 196 (Ohio 1941).
3. Board of Education v. Detroit, 80 Mich. 548, 45 N.W. 585 (1890).
4. Cochran v. Louisiana State Board of Education, 281 U.S. 370, 50 S. Ct. 335 (1930).
5. Everson v. Board of Education, 330 U. S. 1, 67 S.Ct. 504 (1947).
6. Visser v. Noonsack Valley District No. 506, 33 Wash.2d 699, 207 P.2d 198 (1949).
7. Beard v. Board of Education, 81 Utah 51, 16 P.2d 900 (1932).
8. Dalzell v. Bourbon County Board of Education, 135 Ky. 171, 235 S.W. 360 (1921).
9. Board of Education v. Commercial Casualty Insurance Company, 116 W. Va. 503, 182 S.E. 87 (1935).
10. Thomas v. Broadlands School District, 348 Ill. App. 567, 109 N.E.2d 636 (1952).
11. Nohl v. Board of Education, 27 N.M. 232, 199 P. 373 (1921).
12. *Cf.* Wilson v. Graves County Board of Education, 307 Ky. 203, 210 S.W.2d 350 (1948); and *In re* Board of Public Instruction, 160 Fl. 490, 35 So.2d 579 (1948).
13. *Cf.* Taylor v. Board of Public Instruction, 157 Fl. 422, 26 So.2d 180 (1946); and Denny v. Mecklenburg County, 211 N.C. 558, 191 S.E. 26 (1937).
14. Schuerman v. State Board of Education, 284 Ky. 556, 145 S.W.2d 42 (1940).

VII

CONTRACTUAL AUTHORITY
OF SCHOOL BOARDS

IN GENERAL

School boards uniformly have the authority to enter into contracts. The purchase of supplies, employment of teachers, construction of buildings, and all the other very numerous business functions of a board of education could not be carried on in the absence of contractual power. On the other hand, a board of education does not have the freedom of contract enjoyed by individuals or other nongovernmental agencies. It has frequently been stated that boards have only those powers expressly granted them by law or those necessarily implied to enable the board to carry out its express powers. The exact scope of the implied contractual powers of boards cannot be determined as an abstract matter. Indeed, it is frequently impossible to determine whether a particular implied power is held by a board in a specific case until the highest court of the state in which the question arises has determined the question. Not only does the law frequently confer upon boards certain specific powers; it also restricts and limits their contractual authority. Clearly, board authority may not violate constitutional restrictions, such as the constitutional provision forbidding the impairment of the obligation of contract. Among the various specific statutory limitations on board authority are the requirements that certain contracts be in writing, that certain purchases be made and contracts formed only after competitive bids have been received, and the prohibition against entering into contracts in which individual members of the board may have an interest. These and other limitations will be considered presently.

Elements of a Contract

A detailed discussion of all the elements of a contract is beyond the scope of this work. In general, the elements are (1) mutual assent, (2) consideration, (3) legally competent parties, (4) the agreement must not be one prohibited by law, and (5) the agreement must be in the form required by law. Mutual assent means, in effect, that there must be an offer and acceptance; the parties must agree as to the subject matter covered, the price, time of performance, and other similar details. Consideration, to oversimplify the concept, is the price which each side pays for the promise or performance of the other. For example, in a teacher's contract, the consideration which the teacher furnishes is the performance of his duties. The consideration which the board furnishes is the salary paid the teacher. Promises to make gifts or to perform gratuitous services are not supported by consideration and are not contracts. Legally competent parties means simply that the parties must be authorized by law to enter into contractual relations. Obviously, boards of education are not legally competent to enter into all forms of contracts. Certain contracts are beyond their power, and are said to be ultra vires. Certain agreements, such as those to commit a crime, those which offend good morals, and other agreements against public policy, will not be legally sustained. Finally, certain contracts are required to be in writing.

Oral Contracts

Perhaps there is no single point of law upon which there is greater misunderstanding among legal laymen than there is concerning the legal effect or validity of oral contracts. The belief appears quite common that a contract, in order to be legally binding, must be a formal document, drawn in legal language, and signed by the parties thereto. Unless the statute of the state expressly provides that a contract shall be in writing, oral contracts are valid. They may be quite informal and grow out of a number of communications, written or oral, or both. Of course, oral contracts may be difficult to enforce since it may be difficult to prove them unless there were witnesses to all the negotiations out of which it is alleged the oral contract grew. Prudence, therefore, dictates that contracts of importance be reduced to writing and signed by the parties.

There are certain contracts which the law requires to be written in order to be enforceable. A statute known as the Statute of Frauds is in effect in various forms in all states. In general, it provides that contracts for the sale of an interest in land, those which cannot be performed within a year from the making thereof, those made in consideration of marriage, and certain others, shall be in writing in order to be valid. Also, each state has a statute which provides that contracts for the purchase of goods, wares, and merchandise, in excess of a stipulated amount, shall be in writing unless certain other formalities are complied with. This statute varies in detail among the states. It should be checked carefully in order to determine legal limitations on oral contracts in the state concerned.

Personal Interest of Board Members in School Contracts

It is fundamental in the law that a person may not legally represent conflicting interests. For example, an agent may not represent two principals whose interests are in conflict; a lawyer may not legally or ethically represent both parties to a legal controversy; and no public officer may occupy a position which is incompatible with his duties as such officer. The obvious reason for this rule of law is that, human nature being what it is, if there is a conflict between the personal interest of an individual and his duty as a public officer, his self-interest is likely to prevail over his public duty.

For many years courts have been concerned over the fact that unprincipled individuals have been able, by one device or another, to divert public funds to their own use and benefit. A very able court has described the situation in the following language:

> All experience teaches the utter impossibility of wholly preventing unfairness, and advantages taken in the execution of public contracts, even with the most vigilant watchfulness of the public interest. . . . Now, more than ever, do we need a rigid enforcement of public contracts, and a stricter moral discipline, to defeat the varied plans by which money is taken from the treasury without authority. The older we grow as a people, the more systematized and difficult of detection do the schemes become for plundering the public; and among them all, none are more prominent or successful than those which concern contracts and jobs. The very elections of the people are sometimes guided and controlled by the unseen hand of rapacity. Fraudulent claims, fraudulent prices, fraudulent receipts, and fraudulent practices are often winked at or shared in by officials in disregard of honor, honesty, and oaths.[1]

Although many states have statutes which provide that school contracts in which board members have a financial interest are void, or at least voidable at the option of the district, the same conclusion is reached even in the absence of statute. A void contract has no legal effect whatever. A voidable contract is one which is legally valid but which may be declared invalid, that is, avoided, by one of the parties. A contract with a minor is an example of a voidable contract since it may be "avoided" at the option of the minor. Examples of void contracts are those to commit a crime, or others which are against public morals. Statutes on the point vary widely. Some provide merely that it shall be unlawful for public officers to be interested in public contracts. Others impose a criminal penalty upon public officers entering into contracts in the name of the public if they have an interest in them. Still others provide that the acquisition of an interest shall disqualify the officer from holding office. A fairly typical statute on this point is that of Wyoming. It provides:

> It shall not be lawful for any person . . . holding any office . . . under the constitution or laws of this state, to become in any manner interested, either directly or indirectly, . . . in any contract . . . in the making or letting of which such officer may be called upon to act or vote.

In most cases in this area, it appears rather clear that the officer concerned sought to use his position on the board for personal financial gain. In some instances the guilty officer realized that he was violating the law but was willing to assume the risk that his illegal acts would be detected. If a board member, in his individual capacity, sells goods to or performs services for the district for which he is paid, it is clear that his acts are illegal. It is in cases in which he acts for a corporation in which he holds a substantial interest that a great deal of the difficulty arises. It should be noted that a corporation is a separate legal entity, entirely separate and apart from its stockholders and officers. The acts of the officers are, therefore, the acts of the corporation, and not their individual acts. However, courts have made it clear that the interest of a stockholder in a corporation which sells materials to a school district may be such an interest as to render the contract void. On this point the Supreme Court of Wisconsin said:

> It would seem too plain for argument that the . . . [corporation] acquired an interest in the contract . . . and it is equally plain that a person who owns

a large interest in a corporation by reason of his stock therein has a pecuniary interest in the contract. . . . This interest is adverse to the school district, and it is an interest that the clerk of the district had no right to have or acquire. . . . It goes directly against the spirit of the law, as well as the letter of the law.[2]

Contracts in which a board has employed relatives of its members to perform services for the district have been challenged as being in violation of the interest rule. The controversy centers around what constitutes such direct or indirect interest. On this point the cases are in hopeless conflict, and unless the highest court of a state in which the question arises has spoken upon the question, it is not certain what the law is in that state. For example, the courts have been called upon to determine whether a board member has such an interest in a teaching contract between the district and his wife as to bring the contract within the ban of the applicable statute. In a leading case on the point, the Supreme Court of Michigan held that a board member does not have such interest. This court was of the opinion that any wages paid the wife of a member of the board would be her individual property just as they would if she were an entire stranger to the board member.[3] The same conclusion under a similar statute and from similar facts has been reached in Ohio.[4] The Supreme Court of Appeals of West Virginia, under similar facts and statutes, reached the opposite conclusion. Its reasoning was as follows:

> Giving to the various statutes guaranteeing to married women control of their separate estates, and free from the control of the husband, . . . we are still of the opinion that either a husband or a wife, living together as such, has a pecuniary interest in a contract of the other. . . . We prefer to rest our decision on the broad principle that there is still a relation existing between the husband and wife, . . . which creates, on the part of each, an interest in the contracts of the other. . . .[5]

Ultra Vires and Void Contracts

Earlier in this discussion it was pointed out that the school boards and districts do not have unlimited power to contract; that contracts which are beyond the power of the board to make are said to be ultra vires, and are therefore void. However, it does not follow that district contracts are void merely because there may have been legal irregularities in their formation. It is usually held that if a board has the general power to enter into a contract, but its efforts to do so fail because of some irregularity, the contract may subsequently be ratified. Ratification must be effected in the manner prescribed for the making of the contract. For example, if a contract is required to be in writing, but is made orally, it may later be ratified by reducing it to writing. Also, if the law requires that a roll call vote on a contract be taken and this procedure is not followed, ratification of the former acts should be made later through the taking of a roll call vote on the proposition. Another illustration is the situation in which the superintendent of schools purports to enter into a teaching contract with a teacher. Since only the board can enter into formal contracts, the superintendent has thus exceeded his authority. However, if the board subsequently ratifies and validates the action of the superintendent, the contract is as valid as if it had been entered into between the teacher and the board in the first instance. Unfortunately, there is no way to determine in advance, in many cases, the type of defects in purported contracts which the court will classify as mere irregularities. In this uncertain situation, there is no safe substitute for strict compliance with the pertinent legal provisions. However, if there subsequently appears to be some doubt as to the legal regularity of a board action, it should be ratified by the board at the first opportunity. Of course, contracts which are ultra vires, that is, completely beyond the authority of the board to make, cannot be rendered valid through ratification.

The Obligation of Districts to Pay for Goods or Services Received Under Illegal Contracts

Unfortunately, it is not always easy for districts, or those contracting with them, to determine the validity of their contracts prior to the furnishing of goods or the supplying of services under them. In fact, it is not unusual for contracts to be declared void a number of years after the districts have received the goods or services under what all parties thought were legally valid contracts.

The problem is then one of determining whether districts are obliged to pay for the benefits they have received despite the fact that they were provided under an invalid contract. The courts have found this to be a very difficult task. The reason is not far to seek. They are confronted with the situation in which the district will be deprived of part of its legal protection if the case is decided against it, and, on the other hand, the person rendering services or supplying goods will be paid nothing therefor if the decision is against him. Thus, there appears to be no "right" decision. It offends the sense of justice of the courts to permit a district or individual to benefit at the expense of a supplying party. But school funds are public funds, certain legal protection is afforded them, and that protection must not be sacrificed. The conflict between these two fundamental considerations is the source of the difficulty which courts experience in their efforts to reach an equitable decision. From the fact that there is no formal contract it does not necessarily follow that districts are not under any circumstances liable to pay any amount for the goods or services received. Under certain circumstances the law will imply an obligation to pay the *reasonable value* for them. Reasonable value may or may not be the "contract" price. For example, if the "contract" price is $1,000 but it can be proven that the *reasonable value* is only $500, only the latter sum will be recoverable against the district. Under other circumstances, suppliers of goods or services may recover nothing.

Whether boards are bound to pay for services or goods furnished under illegal contracts appears to depend upon whether failure to enter into valid contracts is due to mere irregularity in contracts which the boards had the authority to make. The rule is well stated by the Supreme Court of South Dakota. A contractor had furnished labor and materials in the construction of a school building in that state. South Dakota has a competitive bid law and it was not followed in awarding the contract in question. The court held that there could be no recovery on the contract, since there was no legal one, nor could recovery be had of the reasonable value of the labor and material furnished under the circumstances of this case. In other words, a contract in violation of the competitive bid statute was beyond the power of the board to make; failure to comply with the statute was more than a mere irregularity in the formation of a contract which was within the power of the board. The court said:

> . . . the obligation to do justice rests upon all persons, natural and artificial. . . . Conceding the existence and justice of such a rule, it is without application where the contract is in violation of the express mandatory provisions of a statute. Where a contract is made contrary to a fixed public policy, there can be no implied promise to pay for labor and materials furnished.[6]

It followed that the district retained the benefits without paying any amount for them. It should be observed that the labor and materials in this case became part of a school building which could not be removed without destroying it. Had the contract been for goods or supplies which the district could return to the persons supplying them, it would have been bound to return them.

On the other hand, a case in Illinois involved a situation in which the law requiring that official business be transacted only at a "regular, special or adjourned meeting" had been violated. There it appeared that a salesman had secured written orders for school supplies from two of the three directors privately. Suit on the contract for the price failed. However, the salesman was permitted to recover the reasonable value of the goods since his contract was within the general power of the directors to make so there was an implied contract to pay, not the price, but the reasonable value of the goods.[7]

Contracts Binding Upon Succeeding Boards

Educational policies of a school district normally are determined either by direct action of the people themselves in district-wide meetings or through the board of education for the district. Even the latter case, the citizens retain control of school policy through the ballot box. It follows that any action by an incumbent board which directly or indirectly restricts the action of its successors carries the possibility of thwarting the will of the people. If an incumbent board is legally able to enter into contracts which extend beyond their tenure as board members, they are to that extent able to restrict the power of their successors to change school policy. The question then arises: To what extent, if at all, may an incumbent board "tie the hands" contractually of boards which may have been elected specifically to effectuate a change in district policy? Obviously, the carrying on of school business would be unduly hampered if the law prohibited school boards from entering into any contract which extends into the term of a succeeding board. Thus the problem is to find a reasonable working balance between the extreme of forbidding a board to enter into any contract extending beyond its term, and the other extreme of permitting a board complete freedom in the exercise of contractual power.

The rule is that in the absence of an express or implied statutory limitation on the board's power, it may enter into a contract which does not extend for more than a reasonable time beyond the board's term. Of course, certain long-range financial arrangements, such as bond issues, are expressly authorized by statute. However, these long-range agreements are subject to strict statutory regulation, and boards would be well advised to adhere strictly to the pertinent statutory procedure in such cases. Usual contractual situations, exclusive of those of long range which are expressly permitted by statute, which extend for an unreasonably long period into the term of a succeeding board, have been considered evidence of fraud or collusion in some cases. Of course, if fraud or collusion exists, contracts based thereon are not valid.

While the rule is simple, its application often is far from being so. The difficulty frequently arises when a board is obliged to determine whether there is an implied limitation on its contractual powers to bind succeeding boards. Clearly there is no difficulty if the board's power on the point is "spelled out" in the statutes. A leading case on this problem illustrates the operation of the rule. The case was decided by the Supreme Court of Missouri in 1929. The factual situation which there arose is simple and typical. The board, in December, 1924, employed a teacher to teach a term of school commencing in the next succeeding school year. In April, 1925, a new board member was elected to replace one whose term had expired. At the meeting of the new board in May, 1925, the board repudiated the contract with the teacher and employed another in her stead. The first teacher sued the board on her contract, and her suit was successful. The obvious question was whether the old board could bind the new one on a teacher's contract for the next year. The court held that it could, since the board is a "continuous body or entity." Technically the court is correct as to the nature of a school board. Although it is made up of individual members, the board itself is a separate and distinct entity. It continues in existence unchanged even though its membership changes frequently. On this point the court said:

> The . . . statutes reflect the clear and unmistakable intention of the General Assembly, . . . that the government and control of each of the common school districts . . . shall be vested in a board of directors composed of three members, whose terms of office shall not expire concurrently, but that the term of office of only one of the three members . . . shall expire during

each school year, thereby reflecting the intention of the General Assembly that such governing board . . . shall be a continuous body or entity, of which a majority of the members . . . shall continue in office during the next succeeding year. While provision is made in the statutes for a change in the personnel of the membership of the board of directors . . . yet the intention of the Legislature is clearly reflected . . . that the board . . . is a continuous body or entity, and that transactions had, contracts made with the board, are the transactions and contracts of the board, as a continuous legal entity, and not of the individual members.[8]

Under the law of some states, the power of a board to bind its successor may be automatically restricted by a constitutional or a statutory debt limitation. If the law provides that a school district shall not for any one year become indebted in an amount exceeding the income and revenue provided for that year, the board's contractual power is limited by the statutory or constitutional control of the purse strings. Furthermore, under the law of some states, boards are forbidden to enter into contracts which are to be performed wholly during the term of the succeeding board. This appears to be the law in Iowa under a rather general statute as construed by the Supreme Court of Iowa.[9] In some states the law expressly permits boards to make contracts with school personnel even though the services under the contracts are to be performed wholly within the term of a new board. This is the law in California. The District Court of Appeal in California construed the California statute on this point and held that the board is a "continuing body" that could bind its successors.[10] In view of the uncertainty of the law in this area, boards should check carefully the law in their respective states before entering into a contract which extends beyond the terms of the members of the board.

CONTRACTS WITH PERSONNEL

While contracts with personnel, in common with other contracts, must contain the elements set out earlier in this chapter, there are certain problems of interpretation and enforcement which are peculiar to contracts with school personnel. In this section we will be concerned with some of the more common of these problems, which are frequently litigated.

The Employing Process

Earlier in this chapter it was indicated that the sole contracting agent for the school district is the board of education. Formation of contracts involves the exercise of discretion by the board and this discretion may not be delegated to a committee of the board, or to an employee or officer of the district, such as the superintendent of schools. Ministerial acts, that is, those which are relatively mechanical in nature, and not involving the exercise of discretion, may legally be delegated to others by the board. The reason for this rule is obvious. School board members are elected because the electors of a district have confidence in their judgment and integrity. If it were possible for boards to delegate their discretionary authority to others, the electors would be deprived of the judgment of those they have chosen to exercise it.

In the great majority of districts the exercise of discretion by the board in the employment of personnel consists principally of approving recommendations made by a personnel committee of the board or the superintendent of schools. It is entirely legal for the board to delegate to a committee or the superintendent the task of selecting and recommending to the board that certain personnel be employed. Formal contracts, however, cannot be consummated with personnel except by the board in a legal board meeting. It is quite common, in many areas, for the proper officers of the board, usually the president and secretary, to sign contracts in blank, deliver them to the superintendent of schools, request that he find what he deems to be capable personnel and fill in the names of those he selects for the appropriate vacant positions in the school system. From what has been said above, it follows that this procedure does not result in the formation of a legal contract. Obviously the board could not enter into a contract at the time the officers signed the blank form for the simple reason that it takes two persons or agencies to enter into a contract and only one existed at the time the board officers signed the contract form.

It does not follow that this procedure has no legal significance simply because no valid contract was formed. An illegally formed contract with school personnel may legally be ratified, and thus validated, just as other school contracts may be ratified. The better practice is for a board to ratify "contracts" entered into in behalf of the district by the superintendent of schools, or by the teachers' committee of the board, at the next board meeting. The minutes of the board should clearly describe the contracts in question, and should state clearly that such contracts have been ratified and confirmed. However, personnel contracts may be ratified by circumstances. If school personnel, such as teachers, despite the lack of a valid contract, are permitted to enter upon their duties, this act constitutes as valid a ratification as if it had taken place formally and in a legal meeting of the board. In a few states, among them Connecticut, the law expressly confers upon the superintendent of schools the authority to enter into valid formal contracts with school personnel when expressly authorized to do so by the board.

Duties of Teachers Under Their Contracts

Contracts with teachers vary widely as to the degree of particularity with which the duties of teachers are set out therein. The degree of particularity desirable is a matter upon which there is diversity of opinion. Of course, the name of the teacher, the name of the district, the salary to be paid, when payment shall be made, and the subjects to be taught should be "spelled out" in the contract. Many contracts specify the amount of sick leave, if any, to which the teacher is entitled. Local conditions dictate that certain items be included in teachers' contracts in order to meet certain local problems.

The question as to the extent and scope of a teacher's duties under his contract, beyond the duties expressly stipulated therein, has only fairly recently reached the courts. The question which has long been in the minds of school administrators and teachers is the extent to which a teacher is legally bound to perform his share of the day-to-day tasks which must be performed if the schools are to be a smoothly functioning, successful enterprise. Two recent decisions on this question will indicate the state of the law in this area. The first was decided in New York in 1951. The case involved the validity of certain regulations of the board concerning the work to be required of teachers outside of regular classroom instruction. The teachers were dissatisfied with the regulations and sued to have them annulled. The regulations were sustained but the court established limits as to what legally might be required of teachers outside their classrooms. It made clear that a teacher's work is not restricted to regular school hours. The court, in describing the implied duties of a teacher, said:

> The broad grant of power to fix "duties" of teachers is not restricted to classroom instruction. Any teaching duty within the scope of the license held by a teacher may properly be imposed. The day in which the concept was held that teaching duty was limited to classroom instruction has long since passed. Children are being trained for citizenship and the inspiration and leadership in such training is the teacher. Of course, it is recognized that any by-law of the board outlining teachers' duties must stand the test of reasonableness. Any teacher may be expected to take over a study hall; a teacher engaged in instruction in a given area may be expected to devote part of his day to student meetings where supervision of such teacher is, in the opinion of the board, educationally desirable. Teachers in the field of English and Social Studies and undoubtedly in other areas may be expected to coach plays; physical training teachers may be required to coach both intramural and interschool athletic teams; teachers may be assigned to supervise educational trips which are properly part of the school curriculum. The band instructor may be required to accompany the band if it leaves the building. These are illustrations of some of the duties which boards of education have clear legal justification to require of their employees. A board is not required to pay additional compensation for such services. The duty assigned must be within the scope of the teachers' duties. Teachers may not be required, for instance, to perform janitor service, police service (traffic duty), school bus driving, etc. These are not "teaching duties." The board may not impose upon a teacher a duty foreign to the field of instruction for which he is licensed or employed. A board may not, for instance, require a mathematics teacher to coach intramural teams. Where the service is not part of the duties of a teacher, there is nothing to prevent the board from arranging for such extra service and paying for the same in its discretion.[11]

It will be observed from this quotation that in New York it appears that a teacher may not be required, under his contract, to perform duties for which he is not licensed or employed, with the exceptions noted. This decision greatly restricts the duties which supervisors may assign to teachers.

The second case on this problem arose in California in 1955. There the complaining teacher was chairman of the Social Studies Department in the Sacramento High School. He had attained tenure. During the course of his employment, the teacher had been assigned duties as supervisor of certain school football and basketball games. His assignment was part of the general plan of his superiors to assign to each male member of the faculty the supervision of six athletic events during the school year. Assignments were made impartially and without discrimination. The duties of the supervisor consisted of maintaining order in the student section at games, reporting disturbances to the police, keeping spectators off the field, and other such duties. It will be observed that these duties bore no relationship to the duties of the teacher as chairman of the Social Studies Department. Following the complaint of the teacher, he was transferred from the chairmanship of the Social Studies Department to the position of a full time teacher of English. In lieu of his non-classroom assignments, the teacher was assigned an extra class to teach. In contesting the legal authority of his superiors to assign him the duties described, the teacher did not allege that the change in his duties was by way of reprisal for his failure to perform the "outside" assignments.

Here, as in the New York case, the teacher contended that the non-classroom duties were not called for by his contract. He insisted further that such duties were in the nature of police work, unprofessional in nature, foreign to his field of instruction, and imposed unreasonable hours since some of his assigned outside duties were required to be performed nights, Saturdays and holidays. These, it will be recalled, were the types of duties the New York court held would be outside the teacher's obligations under his contract. The duties he was called upon to perform probably fell within the category which the New York court would call police duties. The District Court of Appeal of California sustained the board's action and held that the assignments complained of were within the implied duties required of the teacher under his contract. The court cited certain statutes to the effect that the board may "prescribe the duties to be performed" by school personnel. However, this board power doubtless exists in the absence of statute. It may plausibly be argued that the court based its decision upon what it deemed may "reasonably" be required of teachers. Its philosophy on the point is expressed in the following language:

> A teacher expects to and does perform a service. . . . If that service from time to time requires additional hours of work, a teacher expects to and does put in extra hours, without thought of measuring . . . compensation in terms of a given sum of money per hour. . . . The direction and super-

vision of extra-curricular activities are an important part of his duties. All of his duties are taken into consideration in his contract for employment at the annual salary. All of this is, of course, subject to the test of reasonableness. . . . What is reasonable must necessarily depend upon the facts of the situation. . . . Supervising the students . . . to protect their welfare at school athletic and social activities . . . is within the scope of the [teacher's] contract. . . .[12]

Thus we find that in California, a teacher, under his contract, may legally be assigned duties quite foreign to his subject matter field. He owes wide general duties to the school in which he works. It would appear that any reasonable assignment would be sustained by the courts. Obviously, this decision affords the school authorities much discretion in assigning teachers to non-academic duties.

Board Regulations as Part of Teachers' Contracts

The rule is well established that boards of education have legal authority to adopt and enforce reasonable rules and regulations for the operation and management of the school system. It follows that if this authority exists all persons connected with the school system, including pupils and teachers, are legally required to obey these rules. Compliance with reasonable rules and regulations of the board is an implied term in all teachers' contracts and the promise so to comply need not be "spelled out" in the contract itself. Teachers generally are bound at their peril to know of the existence and provisions of regulations in existence at the time they sign their contracts.

From what has been said it will be noted that rules and regulations of the board in existence at the date of the employment of the teacher are integral parts of contracts between teachers and boards. The problem then arises as to the legal effect of board regulations and rules adopted after teachers' contracts have been signed. That the signing of these contracts does not limit the rule-making power of the board is, of course, clear. The question is whether rules and regulations adopted after contracts are executed become part of teachers' contracts merely by virtue of such adoption.

In some states, Missouri for example, the answer to this question is contained in express statutory provisions. The applicable section of the law of Missouri is as follows:

The faithful execution of the rules and regulations furnished by the Board shall be considered as part of said teacher's contract: Provided, said rules and regulations are furnished to the teacher by the Board when the contract is made.

It will be noted that under a provision of this type, teachers are not bound by reasonable rules and regulations enacted or adopted by the board after the execution of their contracts. This follows from the provision that copies of the rules and regulations are required to be furnished *"when the contract is made."* In other states, under different statutory provisions, teachers have been held bound by board regulations adopted after contracting as well as by those adopted prior to the contracting. A leading case on this point was decided by the Supreme Court of Indiana. The teacher there involved was on tenure, and his contract contained a provision that the teachers would "obey all rules and regulations of the properly constituted school authorities." It will be noted that this provision makes no distinction between rules adopted before and those adopted after the forming of the contract. In the Indiana case, a teacher announced his candidacy for nomination as state representative. Believing that the best interests of the schools would not be served by this candidacy, the board passed a resolution requiring any teacher who became a candidate for political office to take a leave of absence without pay. After the teacher had been defeated, he sued to recover the amount of salary the board had withheld during his enforced leave. Thus there was squarely presented to the Supreme Court of Indiana the question whether the teacher involved was bound by this subsequently adopted rule of the board. The teacher's suit was unsuccessful. The court said that this rule was a reasonable one and clearly within the rule-making authority of the board. It stated specifically that it is not necessary that the rules or regulations be adopted prior to the execution of a teacher's contract in order that he shall be bound by them. Although the court noted that the teacher's contract contained a promise by him to "observe all rules and regulations of the school authorities," it indicated that the conclusion reached would have been the same had the contract contained no such provision. It would have been "read into" the contract by the court had it not appeared therein. The Supreme Court of Indiana justified its position by emphasizing the educational practicalities of the situation in the following language:

If only such rules could be enforced that were in existence when the contract was signed, the school system might be static for at least one year. New situations could not be met promptly; new problems would have to await solution until the close of the school year. We cannot find any such content in the contract nor in the purpose behind the tenure law. "All rules and regulations" must, we think, include those adopted after as well as those adopted before the execution of the teacher's contract. Any other interpretation would unduly hamper the administration of the public school system by the authorities charged with its management.[13]

Constantly changing conditions in the management of the schools necessitate the modification of rules and regulations to meet them. The greater the flexibility in school administration the more readily the school system may adapt itself to desirable changes. It is highly improbable that teachers will suffer from the rule announced by the Indiana court. Circumstances would be quite unusual if teachers were not afforded adequate protection from capricious and whimsical rules of boards of education by the uniformly recognized requirement that all rules and regulations must meet the test of reasonableness. Statutes such as the Missouri one quoted "freeze" into a teacher's contract, which the teacher is bound to obey, only those rules which were in existence at the contract date and copies of which the teacher has been furnished.

Remedies for Breach of Contract

Normally, the person who breaks a contract is legally obliged to pay the other party to the contract the amount of damages the other party has suffered from the breach. However, there are certain types of cases in which the innocent party is not limited to an action for damages. Rather he may be entitled to have the court require the contract breaker to perform the specific act called for by the contract. This rule is called the rule of specific performance. The types of cases in which the doctrine of specific performance will be applied are rather limited, perhaps the most common being contracts for the sale of land. Specific performance normally will not be granted in personal service contracts. That is, if a contract calls for the performance of personal services, as in the case of teachers' contracts, the law will not enter a judgment at the request of the board requiring the teacher actually to perform his teaching duties according to his contract. By the same token, in the absence of modifying statutes, a teacher who has been illegally discharged by the board can bring an action for damages, but would not be entitled to a decree requiring the board to permit the teacher to remain in his position.

It is clear that in many, if not in most, cases, payment of damages by the board does not afford an adequate remedy to illegally discharged teachers. In view of this fact, tenure laws of several states expressly provide that an illegally discharged teacher may require the board to restore him to the position from which he has been illegally discharged. The reason for these provisions is clear. Even if a teacher has been illegally discharged, his professional reputation and standing probably suffer some damage. Perhaps the best judicial justification for applying the rule that an illegally discharged teacher is entitled to be restored to his position was expressed by the Supreme Court of Missouri. A superintendent of schools was threatened with illegal dismissal. He refused to submit to the board's action, and insisted on continuing his functions as superintendent of schools. The superintendent then sought a order from the court enjoining the board from dismissing him from his position. The injunction was granted and he was ordered reinstated in his position. The basis of the decision is as follows:

> . . . real argument could be made that the wrong threatening the plaintiff [superintendent] is amenable so little to market-place responses that he ought not to be turned out of equity with the comfortless instruction that the blow that is about to fall on him is one he must receive before he can have any redress at all and then have only that which an award of money can administer. Dismissed from his post of honor and responsibility, a professional teacher is stigmatized, sometimes beyond rehabilitation, before his colleagues, before those who might otherwise want his professional services, and before the public generally. . . . Injunction, we think, is an available and appropriate remedy to prevent plaintiff's dismissal, and we so rule.[14]

It is vital to those in the professions that they "keep their hands in" in their respective professions. A teacher, for example, may become out-of-date rather quickly after he stops teaching. That the payment of damages or salary to the teacher for the balance of his contract term is quite an inadequate remedy for his illegal dismissal is clear. Teacher dismissals, legal or illegal, are often the subject of wide discussion throughout the community and very frequently beyond the confines of the district.

Even if a teacher is illegally discharged, many, if not most, of his prospective future employers may be quite unaware of the fact of the illegality of his discharge. There may be a tendency to brand him as a troublemaker or otherwise undesirable. Under these cirmumstances, it would not be surprising if the teacher in question should, in many instances, be obliged to accept a lower position than the one from which he was illegally discharged. In the view of the Missouri court, these hardships which an illegally discharged teacher may be obliged to suffer, are sufficient justification for requiring the board to reinstate the teacher in his position.

Duty of an Illegally Discharged Teacher to Mitigate His Damages

It is a well-established rule of law that a person entitled to sue for breach of contract may not build up his damages. On the contrary, there is a positive responsibility upon him to mitigate, that is, lessen, the damages he may have suffered from the breach. Under this rule, an illegally discharged teacher is not entitled to sit idly by and recover his salary. He is required to make reasonable efforts to procure another position. However, he is not obliged to accept a position of less dignity and standing than the one from which he is illegally discharged. The question as to what lines of work will, by the courts, be held to be not inferior to teaching may be a difficult one in some cases. The law also recognizes that some teaching positions are inferior to others. Neither is a teacher obliged to accept a position in a distant community in order to mitigate the damages which he has suffered.

A single recent case will illustrate the operation of the mitigation of damages rule. A teacher in a Pennsylvania district was held to have been illegally discharged. It was agreed at the trial in the lower court that the teacher had been employed as a teacher elsewhere during the period in question at a salary higher than that provided in the contract with the district which had illegally discharged him. The Superior Court of Pennsylvania held that the teacher was entitled only to nominal damages and awarded him $1.00. In its opinion that court quoted with approval the following reasoning of the lower court:

"To set off or credit, against the salary owing to an improperly dismissed teacher, compensation earned by the teacher from other employers during the period of such improper dismissal does not in any way abate the salary or compensation to which he is entitled under his contract for he receives that salary or compensation, either wholly from the school district or wholly or partly from others. He is in exactly the same position, so far as compensation is concerned, as if he had not been improperly dismissed. Improper dismissal is a breach of contract for which the employee may recover damages. Damages are the loss suffered by one person by reason of a breach of contract on the part of another and if the school teacher received the same compensation for his work during the period of improper dismissal as he would have received if he had continued in the position from which he was improperly dismissed, he has suffered no damages except such as may arise from matters following other elements than loss of salary." [15]

It is important to note that in mitigation of damages cases, the burden is upon the board to prove that the teacher in question did not use reasonable efforts to mitigate his damages, rather than the burden being upon the teacher to prove that he did use such reasonable efforts. In speaking of the mitigation rule as it applies to this point, the Supreme Court of Appeals of West Virginia said:

> The rule, however, does not require him [the teacher] to show such diligence. He may rest his case upon proof of a valid contract and its breach, the measure of the damages being the contract price of his services. Mitigation of damages is an affirmative defense, and its burden is entirely on the contract breaker. [16]

The "Contract Jumper" Problem

Assuming a valid contract has been formed between a school board and a teacher, the question arises whether the board in fact has any assurance, despite the contract, that the teacher will appear for duty when school opens. Unfortunately, a small but troublesome minority of teachers throughout the country enter into contracts and use the security of position thereby afforded merely as an "insurance policy" while seeking a more desirable position. If one is offered to such a teacher, he does not hesitate to accept it and resign his first position, despite the fact that the board of the first district may have little or no time to fill the position before the opening of school.

What, then, may a board legally do in order to protect itself from such contract jumpers? It has often been said that a contract between a teacher and a board is one-sided. Technically, this is not true, since a teacher who breaks his contract with a board is as liable to pay damages as is an individual who breaks his contract with the district to construct a school building. As a practical matter, however, there is much to support the statement that teachers' contracts are one-sided. No cases have come to our attention in which a board of education has brought an action against a teacher for damages because he has broken his contract with the board. Possible reasons are: (1) a teacher would probably not be very effective if he felt obliged to remain in a teaching position under threat of a lawsuit in the event of his resignation; (2) as a practical matter, it would probably be quite difficult for the board to prove the amount of damages it has sustained as a result of a teacher breaking his contract; (3) the time and expense of a lawsuit might prevent the board from instituting one; and (4) until fairly recent years most teachers probably would be "judgment proof" by virtue of financial inability to pay if judgment should be rendered against them. On the other hand, cases in which teachers have sued boards for damages as a result of their being illegally dismissed by the board are very numerous indeed. In recognition of the fact that boards have no practical and feasible remedy against contract-jumping teachers, many boards paying teachers in twelve monthly payments include in teachers' contracts a provision that if a teacher should resign within a stated number of days before school opens, frequently about thirty days, the last month's salary shall not be paid to the teacher. As far as we are aware, the legality of such a contractual provision has not reached a court of last resort. If a teacher should contest it, the contest probably would be based upon the contention that the provision is a penalty, and the law normally does not enforce contractual penalties. However, in the absence of any authority on the point, it is our opinion that such a contractual provision probably would be judicially sustained. In some states, by statute or by rule of the state board of education or the state department of education, a contract-jumping teacher is not permitted to teach in the state in question during the period covered by the first contract if he breaks that contract.

NON-PERSONNEL CONTRACTS

Although all contracts have certain essential elements in common, special considerations arise in many instances by virtue of the fact that not all contracts deal with the same subject matter. This was observed in the previous section dealing with school personnel contracts. In this section we shall concern ourselves with problems which arise in school contracts generally, but which normally are not involved in contracts with school personnel.

Competitive Bid Requirement

Quite generally, legislatures are convinced that public agencies, such as school districts, will receive greater value for their money if certain contracts are awarded on the basis of competitive bids. Statutes of this type usually provide that certain contracts, usually those in excess of a stipulated amount, shall be awarded to the "lowest responsible bidder" or "lowest and best bidder."

Interpretation of the two quoted phrases has been rendered by a number of courts. The obvious question is: What constitutes the "lowest responsible bidder" or the "lowest and best bidder"? Of course, the determination of which bidder is lowest is simple, since it may be accomplished by inspection of the bid amounts. However, there is no doubt that it was the legislative intent that other qualities of bidders should be taken into account; otherwise the word "competent" or the word "best" in the statute would be meaningless. Among the cases most frequently cited and quoted from on this problem is one decided by the Supreme Court of Pennsylvania. There it appeared that the board of education had awarded a contract for the construction of a school building to the fourth lowest bidder, without investigating the responsibility of the three lower ones. The Pennsylvania statute was the common one which directs that certain contracts be awarded to the "lowest responsible bidder." Suit was brought by interested persons to enjoin the work on the contract alleging that it had not been let according to legal requirements. The court granted the injunction because no investigation as to the responsibility of the three lower bidders had been made. In discussing the qualities of bidders which the board may take into account in determining who is the lowest responsible bidder the court said:

> The term "lowest responsible bidder" does not mean the lowest bidder in dollars; nor does it mean the board may capriciously select a higher bidder regardless of responsibility or cost. What the law requires is the exercise of sound discretion by the directors. They should call to their assistance

the means of information at hand to form an intelligent judgment. They should investigate the bidders to learn their financial standing, reputation, experience, facilities, judgment, and efficiency as builders. This was not done. . . . Though the directors were not bound in law to give the contract to the lowest bidder, who might be irresponsible, they were bound to investigate, and if the bidder measured up to the law's requirement as a responsible party, the board could not capriciously award the contract to another. . . . There should be a sufficient reason, where a bidder is lowest and responsible, why the job was not given to him.[17]

Regrettably, local politics play, or are alleged to play, a part in the letting of school contracts in some cases. When school boards permit political considerations to creep into their management of the school system, they are inviting legal difficulty. For example, in a school district in Ohio, the board had awarded a school contract to one who was not the lowest bidder despite the fact that the usual legal requirement as to such letting appears in the law of Ohio. It happened that the lowest bidder had opposed certain members of the board in the school election, and he alleged that this influenced the board in the letting of the contract. Of course the board denied any such influence. These circumstances placed the board in a very unenviable position. It was almost certain to be accused of playing politics with school contracts if it failed to award the contract to the lowest bidder even though there was substantial evidence of his lack of responsibility. The Court of Appeals of Ohio recognized the dilemma in which the board found itself. On the matter of the alleged opposition of the bidder to the board, the court said:

This should have made it a delicate matter for the board to reject . . . [the lowest bidder's] bid, and this fact tends to complicate what would otherwise be a reasonably clear state of facts. While it would be an outrage to deny a contract to . . . [the lowest bidder] because he was politically opposed to the members of the board of education, it would be equally wrong to use that fact to secure for him a more favorable consideration than a stranger would have.[18]

However, the board had adequate reasons in this case for denying the contract to the lowest bidder. He had performed other services for the district and his work had been found quite unsatisfactory. He had declined to correct certain defects in his work, and had proven to be a rather difficult person with whom to work. All these matters may properly be taken into account by the board in determining who is the "lowest responsible bidder."

If a board refuses to award a contract to the lowest bidder, it is usually not legally obliged to explain to the lower bidders why the contract was not awarded to them. Neither is an unsuccessful bidder whose bid was the lowest entitled to a hearing on the matter. Although this appears to be the general rule, it is not applicable in all states.

Mistaken Bids

The reader might be surprised at the number of cases in which bidders have discovered large mistakes in their bids after they have been submitted. There are cases for instance in which a bidder has, through mistake, failed to include in the computation of his bid the cost of installing a heating system. In another, although it was not a school case, the contractor had figured the floor covering in a building an entire story short. Closer examination of the pressure under which contractors work as the deadline for submitting bids approaches, reveals circumstances which are very conducive to the making of mistakes. Perhaps the most common mistakes are mistakes in computation and failures to include certain items which the specifications call for. The making of mistakes is understandable when it is recognized that there is much "jockeying for position," by competing contractors, and between subcontractors and the principal contractor himself. Contractors prefer to submit their bids at the latest possible moment in order to take into account any last minute changes in prices of materials and services which will be required in performing the contract. By the same token, subcontractors prefer to submit their bids to the main contractor as near the deadline as possible in order to prevent the contractor from having time in which to obtain a lower bid from some other subcontractor. The result is that often the main contractor has very limited opportunity, or possibly no opportunity, to run a final check on his figures before submitting his bid.

Lawsuits arise in such cases when the board accepts the mistaken bid and the contractor refuses to enter into a contract on the basis of the bid submitted. The legal rule in such cases is that if the board knows, or has reason to know, that a mistake has been made in the contractor's bid, it may not accept the bid. If one bid is grossly out of line with the others, the board might well be put on notice of the possibility that the bidder has made a mistake. Certainly if the board does note or reasonably should have noted mistakes in computation, it may not hold a bidder to his bid. Good faith and honest dealing are required in such cases. On the other hand, if the board accepts the mistaken bid in good faith and without reason to know that a mistake has been made, and if there are certain other equitable considerations which would make it unfair to others to excuse the contractor's mistake, the contractor will be held legally liable if he refuses to enter into a contract upon the basis of his bid.

Changes in Contracts

In contracts for buildings of substantial size, it is a virtual impossibility to foresee, in detail, every desirable feature which the building should contain. The question then arises whether the board and contractor legally may agree to changes in a contract which was awarded under competitive bids, without readvertising for bids. The practicalities involved in building construction would indicate that boards and contractors should have a certain amount of freedom to agree to small and relatively unimportant changes in the contract specifications. On the other hand, if they have unlimited authority to make changes after contracts have been let, the protection afforded the public by competitive bid statutes might well be destroyed. The problem, then, is to find some sort of reasonable working arrangement between these two extremes. That is precisely what the courts have sought to do.

In the Pennsylvania competitive bid case referred to above, the board and contractor, after the contract had been let under the competitive bid statute, decided to use a little more expensive brick than that specified in the contract. The cost of the building was thereby increased, but there is no evidence that the increase was great. In sustaining the legality of the agreed change without readvertising for bids, the court said:

> That the directors later decided to use a little more expensive brick would not condemn the letting. . . . There was no such departure from the general purpose as would require reletting. Unforeseen contingencies or new ideas sometimes make it necessary to change the character or quality of material or a part of the structure from the original plans. A certain flexibility in the power of officials to take care of these matters is intended [by the law] to be granted, that the law relating to public letting may not become

an instrument of oppression through a too rigid construction. These officers must act honestly, reasonably, and intelligently, and a new departure must not so vary from the original plan or be of such importance as to constitute a new undertaking . . . where fairness could only be reached through competitive bidding. Courts, however, will be slow to interfere unless it appears the officers were not acting in good faith.[19]

A case in which agreed changes between the board and the contractor exceeded the limit which the law will permit arose in South Dakota. The contract there involved contained a provision which permitted the board to authorize changes in the work or materials to be furnished. While the school building was under construction, the board decided to construct a stage opening which had not been specified in the original contract. The board did not advertise for bids for the stage opening and none were received. A proposal was received from the general building contractor to do the job for the additional sum of $1,761.00. The original contract price of the building was $33,975.00. The proposal of the general contractor was accepted and the work was completed, including the stage opening. The legality of the agreement for the construction of the stage opening was challenged on the ground that there had been no advertising for bids for the job. The Supreme Court of South Dakota held the contract was invalid. It stated that construction contracts may contain provisions which permit changes incidental to the complete execution of the work described in the contract. They may not, however, authorize supplementary contracts for distinct and independent work. In other words, agreed changes may not be so great as to constitute a new and independent job. However, the right to make incidental changes in contracts does not depend upon that right being reserved in the contracts as was done in the South Dakota case. The right exists independently of such reservation.

Architects' Certificates

In school construction cases, the common practice is to employ an architect, not only to prepare the plans and specifications, but also to supervise the construction of the building. The architect is thus the representative of the board of education with the duty of seeing that the contractor constructs the building according to plans and specifications. If the project is a sizable one, it is common practice to provide in the contract that progress payments shall be made to the contractor as construction progresses. In the absence of a provision in the contract to that effect, the contractor is not entitled to partial payments during the period of construction. He is obliged to complete the building according to plans before he is entitled to payment of any amount. When progress payments are provided for, it is common practice to require the contractor to present a certificate of the architect certifying that the amount and quality of work entitling the contractor to a partial payment has been performed as the contract requires.

The architect's certificate requirement has raised a number of very troublesome problems. The legal rule is that the certificate must be procured as a condition precedent to the right to receive payment, unless production of the certificate is, on some basis, excused by the law. A hard and fast requirement that the contractor procure the certificate may result in great hardship. The builder has constructed the building on the land of the school district, and it may not legally be removed by him. Under these circumstances the district would be enriched at the expense of the contractor, a state of affairs which offends the sense of justice.

In order to alleviate this hardship, the law excuses the builder from presenting the certificate under certain circumstances. He is excused from producing it if the architect has died or become incapacitated and thus unable to execute a certificate. Of course, the contractor is excused if the architest's refusal to grant the certificate is the result of collusion with the board or the architect is otherwise guilty of fraud or bad faith. It is implied in such contracts that the certificate need not be produced if it can be shown that the architect did not exercise an honest judgment in determining whether the contractor's performance is in accordance with the contractual specifications.

Acceptance of Defective Performance

Despite the supervision of construction by the architect, defective performance by the contractor sometimes may not be detected until performance has been certified as complete and the contractor is entitled to final payment. Even though the architect may have overlooked certain defects in construction and has issued a certificate to the contractor certifying that the building has been constructed according to specifications, the district has an action against the contractor for breach of contract if it is able to show that performance was in fact incomplete or defective. The remedy of the district for breach of contract probably would not be as prompt and speedy as the board of education might desire. As a practical matter, correction of defective performance frequently can be obtained more promptly if the board is legally entitled to rescind its previous acceptance of defective performance in reliance on the architect's certificate and withhold final payment to the contractor until he corrects his mistakes.

Precisely this question recently arose in New York. There it appeared that the board had approved a resolution certifying that the work had been performed according to contract, and that the contractor was entitled to final payment. Later it appeared that the acceptance was erroneous, and the board sought to rescind the acceptance. The court held that not only did the board have the right to rescind its acceptance under the circumstances described, but in fact had the duty to do so.[20]

Finally, on the matter of acceptance of performance, it appears that a board, either itself or through its inspector, is not bound to supervise construction at the risk of being held to have accepted defective performance if supervision is not provided. A recent case which arose in California involved this question. The contract called for a certain degree of soil compaction in connection with the construction of a school building. The district's inspector thought the contractor was compressing the soil as required, but he made no test to determine the amount of soil compaction. This did not excuse the contractor. The Appellate Court of California said, on this point:

> The mere fact that the inspector thought that the back-filling was being done properly does not . . . [prevent the district] from requiring that the compaction meet the tests specified [in the contract]. The trial court found as follows: "The day to day inspection performed . . . did not constitute approval or ratification of the work improperly done by the [contractor]." . . .[21]

Good practice dictates that close inspection of construction by the district architect be insisted upon as the building progresses. Even if there is no legal obligation to provide that inspection, it is far easier to procure complete performance if errors are detected and corrected promptly during construction. It is entirely possible that under certain circumstances the presence of a district architect on the job might tend to discourage an unprincipled contractor from careless or intentional "cutting of corners." Furthermore, ethical contractors will usually appreciate the opportunity to correct errors during construction since correction is usually much less expensive then than it is after the building is completed.

Liquidated Damages

It is common practice for the parties to a contract to agree that a certain sum shall be paid in case of breach of the contract. Such provisions are usually referred to as liquidated damages clauses. The purpose of these clauses is to set, in advance of any breach of a contract, by a agreement of the parties, the amount of damages which shall be paid in case the contract is broken by either party. In the absence of such a contractual provision, the amount of damages which one who breaks a contract would be obliged to pay would be determined in a lawsuit by a jury, or by a judge if the case is tried before a judge without a jury. It is ordinarily prudent to insert liquidated damages clauses in contracts involving substantial amounts. Since the parties to the contract are familiar with the subject matter involved, they are in a better position than either a jury or a judge to determine what damages reasonably may be expected to flow from a breach of the contract.

While true liquidated damages clauses have been uniformly sustained by the courts, it does not follow that all clauses so designated will be judicially upheld. A clause, even though designated as a liquidated damages clause, which is in fact a penalty, will be stricken down by the courts. In some cases, it is a question of some nicety whether a particular clause is in fact a liquidated damages clause or provides for a penalty. In general, the rule is that if the contract is for performance of uncertain value and a sum is fixed to be paid for breach of it, and if the sum so fixed is not greatly in excess of the probable damages which reasonably might result from the breach, the provision will be sustained as a liquidated damages clause. On the other hand, if the amount of damages fixed by the parties exceeds those which may reasonably be expected to flow from the breach, the clause will be held to provide for a penalty, and will be stricken from the contract. If the clause is held to be a penalty, the contract then stands as if no clause on the damages point had been included in it. In the light of this situation, if the parties decide to include a liquidated damages clause in their contract, they should be as certain as possible that the amount of damages they set reasonably approximates the amount of damages which probably would flow from a breach of the contract.

CITATIONS

1. Hague v. City of Philadelphia, 48 Pa. 527 (1865).
2. Bissell Lumber Co. v. Northwestern Casualty and Surety Co., 189 Wis. 343, 207 N.W. 697 (1926).
3. Thompson v. District Board, 252 Mich. 629, 233 N.W. 439 (1930).
4. Board of Education v. Boal, 104 Ohio St. 482, 135 N.E. 540 (1922).
5. Haislip v. White, 124 W.Va. 633, 22 S.E.2d 361 (1942).
6. Seim v. Independent Dist. of Monroe, 70 S.D. 315, 17 N.W.2d 342 (1945).
7. Sebastian v. School Directors, 313 Ill. App. 652, 30 N.E.2d 565 (1942).
8. Tate v. School Dist. No. 11, 324 Mo. 477, 23 S.W.2d 1013 (1929).
9. Independent School Dist. v. Pennington, 181 Ia. 933, 105 N.W. 209 (1917).
10. King Union High School Dist. v. Waibel, 2 Cal. App.2d 65, 37 P.2d 861 (1934).
11. Parrish v. Moss, 106 N.Y.S.2d 577 (1951).
12. McGrath v. Burkhard, 131 Cal.App.2d 367, 280 P.2d 864 (1955).
13. School City of East Chicago v. Sigler, 219 Ind. 9, 36 N.E.2d 760 (1941).
14. LeMasters v. William, 281 S.W.2d 580 (Mo. 1955).
15. Coble v. School Dist. of Twp. of Metal, 116 A.2d 113 (Pa. 1955).
16. Martin v. Board of Education of Lincoln County, 120 W.Va. 621, 199 S.E. 887 (1938).
17. Hibbs v. Arensberg, 276 Pa. 24, 119 A. 727 (1923).
18. Hudson v. Board of Education, 41 Ohio App. 402, 179 N.E. 701 (1931).
19. Hibbs v. Arensberg, *supra* note 17.
20. Application of Caristo Construction Corp., 152 N.Y.S.2d 259 (1956).
21. Pacific Coast Builders v. School Dist., 300 P.2d 309 (Cal. App. 1956).

VIII

SCHOOL BOARD MEMBERSHIP
AND MEETINGS

SCHOOL BOARD MEMBERSHIP

Eligibility for Board Membership

Since board members are state officers the legislature has the authority to specify what persons shall be eligible for board membership. Although the problem does not seem to have arisen frequently, it appears that board members must be individuals, and not corporations, such as banks, trust companies, and the like.

Eligibility requirements for school board membership differ from state to state. In some states the constitution provides that all qualified electors shall be eligible to hold office. Of course, in a state in which this constitutional provision appears, the legislature would be without authority to prescribe other eligibility requirements. In the absence of constitutional limitations, the legislatures have wide discretion in determining who shall be eligible for board membership. Very few qualifications are required in the various states of those who seek to become board members. Approximately 85 per cent of local board members are popularly elected, and determination of those best fitted for board membership is left largely to the local electorates. Among the requirements in some states are residence within the district, the ownership of property within the district, and payment of taxes within the district.

Holding of Incompatible Offices

That public officers may not hold incompatible offices is well established. The purpose of the rule is obvious. It is designed to prevent an individual from holding two or more offices the duties of which may be in conflict, that is, incompatible. The states generally have constitutional and statutory provisions, more or less detailed, dealing with the problem. Many states have statutes expressly declaring certain offices incompatible. For example, the New York law provides that "a trustee or a member of a board of education vacates his office by the acceptance of either the office of district superintendent or of supervisor." However, even if there is no controlling statute on the point, the holding of incompatible offices is forbidden by the common law.

The determination of what constitutes incompatibility of offices is often difficult. While there are numerous judicial statements as to what will render offices incompatible, there are many cases in which it is impossible to predict whether the court will hold the offices in question compatible or incompatible. Perhaps the following language from an early New York case on what constitutes incompatibility of offices is as clear a statement as any:

> When one office is not subordinate to the other, nor the relations of the one to the other such as are inconsistent and repugnant, there is not that incompatibility from which the law declares that the acceptance of one is the vacation of the other. The force of the word, in its application to this matter is, that from the nature and relations to each other, of the two places, they ought not to be held by the same person, from the contrariety and antagonism which would result in the attempt by one person to faithfully and impartially discharge the duties of one, toward the incumbent of the other. . . . The offices must subordinate, one the other, and they must, *per se*, have the right to interfere, one with the other, before they are incompatible at common law.[1]

Tests, then, of incompatibility are whether one office is subordinate to the other and whether the holder of the offices would be unable to perform his duties under one office without violating his duties under the other.

The incompatible office holding problem has been considered frequently in Texas. Many of the cases have arisen from the fact that under Texas law a district may elect to have its school taxes assessed and collected by its own collector. Apparently it has not been uncommon in that state for a district to appoint as its collector the collector for the city or the county. A single Texas case will illustrate the point. About two weeks after a collector for the district had been appointed, he was elected Sheriff and Tax Collector for the county. The collector defaulted and suit was brought against his sureties for the amount lost by the district. The defense of the sureties was that the collector had accepted and qualified for the office of Sheriff and County Collector; that he had thereby immediately vacated the office of District Collector; and that the default thus occurred after the collector had ceased to be District Collector, for which default they were not liable. In other words, it was the position of the sureties that the offices of sheriff and tax collector for the district were incompatible, and that the collector had ceased to be collector of taxes for the district immediately upon his being elected and qualified for the position of sheriff. In the suit brought against the collector's sureties for the loss suffered by the district, the Supreme Court of Texas agreed with the contention of the sureties, and held them not liable for the collector's default.[2]

In some states the acceptance of an incompatible office does not automatically create a vacancy in the first office. This is true in states having statutes which provide that a person elected or appointed to office shall serve in that office until his successor is elected or appointed and qualified. The state of New Mexico has such a statute, and the supreme court of that state interpreted it in a case involving a number of important points. The facts were that a member of the board had been appointed clerk of the board, in which position she served for two years or more. Under New Mexico law, the clerk of a board of education is entitled to receive certain compensation. Suit was brought by the state to oust her from membership on the board on the ground that membership was incompatible with the position of clerk. The court held that the offices were incompatible, but that the statute which provides that a person elected or appointed to an office shall serve in that office until his successor is elected or appointed and qualified, enabled the board member to remain in her position on the board until her successor was elected and qualified, despite the incompatibility of the offices.[3] Thus, since no successor to her had been selected, the suit to oust her failed. The reason for the rule is that public convenience should not be permitted to suffer from vacancies in public offices if it can be avoided.

In some states, by express provision of statute, the holding of one office by the incumbent of certain other offices, automatically vacates the first office held. New York is one such state, and the application of the statute may be shown by reference to a decision of a New York court. It appeared that a board member had been elected to the office of town supervisor. His term as supervisor was to commence on January 1, 1952. He did not resign from his membership on the school board until April 2, 1952. On April 5, 1952, the district superintendent of schools appointed a successor on the board as he had a right to do under New York law. That law provides that unless an action to fill a board vacancy is called within thirty days after it occurs, the superintendent of schools may fill the vacancy by appointment. The legal validity of the appointment was challenged. The challengers insisted that the vacancy on the board of school trustees occurred on April 2, the date of the resignation of the member. If this contention is sustained, the superintendent had no authority to appoint the successor until thirty days after that date. On the other hand, if the vacancy occurred automatically when the member accepted the office of supervisor, the statutory thirty days had expired, and the superintendent had the legal power to choose a successor. The New York court held that the vacancy occurred when the member accepted the office of supervisor.[4] The legal provision controlling the matter is as follows:

> A trustee or a member of a board of education vacates his office by the acceptance of either the office of district superintendent or of supervisor.

We thus find that in some states the acceptance of a specified office by an officer may automatically constitute vacation of another office held by him regardless of whether or not the two offices in question are incompatible.

Board Vacancies

Vacancies on boards of education may, of course, result from many causes. We have just considered the situation in which a vacancy may occur as a result of an incumbent member accepting an incompatible position. Of course, board vacancies may be created when members are removed for misfeasance or malfeasance in office. This point will be considered more fully later in Chapter X. Aside from these situations, vacancies may occur because of death, resignation, or abandonment of the position through failure to attend meetings and discharge the responsibilities of the office. Vacancies may also occur as a result of a board member removing from the district when the law requires residence in the district as a legal condition of board membership. This situation has reached the courts so frequently that it will be given special consideration here.

The chief difficulty in the removal cases is that of determining when or whether a board member has ceased to be a legal resident of the district. This question is related to the familiar one of what constitutes residence in a school district for voting purposes. In that connection the courts have emphasized the importance of intention in determining the matter of legal residence. We find the same consideration involved in the board vacancy cases. A relatively recent case, decided by the Court of Civil Appeals of Texas, illustrates the difficulty which arises in these matters. The trustees of a school district sought to enjoin another trustee from acting in that capacity on the ground that he had vacated his office. The Constitution of Texas provides that if an officer removes from the county and establishes his residence elsewhere, he thereby vacates his office. Under Texas law a trustee of an independent school district is a county officer; thus this constitutional provision applies to him.

It appears that on August 4, 1954, the board member against whom the injunction was sought sold his home in one county and moved to another county. There he took employment as a salesman. He stayed there about a month and then moved back to the first county. The remaining board members insisted that his removal, the taking of his family to the second county, entering his children in school there, and the selling of his house in the first county, constituted vacating his board membership. On the other hand, the board member testified that he did not intend to, and did not in fact, permanently change his residence from the first county. He said that his new position was purely on a trial basis, that he intended to return to his original home if that position did not prove satisfactory. The question, then, is whether under these circumstances the board member had removed from the county and thereby vacated his position on the board.

The court held that the board member had legally removed from the county and had vacated his position. It recited the familiar rule on "residence," namely, when a person voluntarily takes up his abode in a given place without any present intention to remove therefrom, such place of abode becomes his residence or home. Although it may actually have been the intention of the member to return to the first county at some future time, he had in fact established his residence in the second county. The court said:

> It appears that when . . . [the board member] took up his residence, either temporary or permanent, in . . . [the second county], with his wife and children living with him . . . with no present intention then formed in his mind to return to . . . [the first county], he became a resident of . . . [the second county] and he vacated his office as a member of the . . . [school board]. His intention to move back . . . if his job . . . proved unsatisfactory does not have any significance, since it was not a fixed intention, not a formed or present intent to return to . . . [the first county], but was at most an intent subject to a future contingency.[5]

Thus, what constitutes removal from the district depends upon the circumstances of the case. Perhaps it is accurate to say that selling one's house and moving to another school district is almost conclusive of legal removal. In fact, in an earlier Texas case, it was held that selling a home and moving from it to another district is an abandonment of board membership as a matter of law.[6] That is to say, these acts would be deemed to be so clear as to the intention of the removing party that he would be held to have removed from the district regardless of what his unexpressed intention may have been. It is clear that one cannot acquire or change his residence by intention alone, although intention certainly is important in such matters. Intention must be accompanied by some act implementing the intention. It is entirely possible that one's actions, or his failure to act, may speak far more eloquently regarding his intention than any words could do. From what has just been said it must not be concluded that removal from a district, if accompanied by circumstances clearly showing no intention to remove therefrom, will always be held to be a legal removal. In one case it appeared that the home of a board member had burned and he had moved his family across the line into another district until he could reestablish his home in the first district. In fact, it appears that the board member did not realize that he had moved across the district line. Under these circumstances it was found by the court that there had not been such removal from the district as to constitute abandonment by the removing board member of his position on the board.[7]

Filling of Board Vacancies

Since the legislature has the authority to determine how board members shall be elected in the first instance, it follows that it may also specify the manner in which vacancies on the board shall be filled. Although the statutes on the point vary from state to state, the usual plans for filling vacancies are by special elections, appointment by the remaining members of the board, or appointment by a state agency such as the state board of education, or by a state official such as the state superintendent of public instruction or the governor of the state. Statutes on this point in the state in which the question arises should be checked very carefully since the courts are quite uniform in holding that vacancies in school offices may be filled only as the statutes provide.

A very substantial amount of litigation has arisen in cases in which the remaining members of the board on which the vacancy has occurred seek to fill that vacancy by appointment when permitted to do so by law. Inherent in this problem are all the difficulties involved in other situations in which actions of the board are challenged, such as lack of quorum, illegal meeting of the board, and many others. An illustration of the legal difficulties involved when board members seek to fill a vacancy on the board is a case which arose in Kentucky. At a regular school election five members of the board were elected. A series of difficulties arose which resulted in the preferring of charges against the board members by the state board of education, and a number of the board members resigned before the proceedings against them had been commenced. A number of other persons had been either elected or appointed to membership on the board and the usual challenges and counter challenges were made by various persons and groups as to the legality of office-holding by a number of the individuals concerned. Finally, in what may have been a move born of desperation, the governor of the state appointed members to fill the various vacancies. Only a single board member was conceded to have been legally selected and thus to hold his office by legal authority. The right of the governor to fill the vacancies was challenged, and under the statutes and constitution of Kentucky the Court of Appeals held that the governor had no authority to make the appointments. The statute permitted the filling of vacancies on boards of education by appointment by the other members of the board:

Any vacancy in any board of education, from whatever cause occurring, shall be filled for the unexpired term by the other members of the board within 90 days after such vacancy occurs, and in case the vacancy is not filled by the other members of the board within said 90-day period, it shall be filled by the state board of education.

Thus it was determined by the Court of Appeals that the governor had no authority to act in the matter, and that under this statute the only authority to fill vacancies was by other members of the board if they acted within ninety days after the vacancy occurred. As above stated, there was in office only one legally and duly elected member of the board at all times when the vacancies were attempted to be filled by the selection of the persons whose right to hold office was challenged. The question then arises whether the words "other members" in the statute may be construed to mean a single member. That is, may the single remaining member appoint the other four members of the board for the unexpired terms of the members who had been removed from the board?

In sustaining the authority of the single remaining board member to make the appointments under this statute, the court referred to its holding in a previous case and said:

Adhering to our construction of the words "other members" as used in the statute construed in that case, vacancies in membership of the board may be filled by the "other members," whether one or more of them constitute the "other members" at the time of the filling the vacancy or vacancies, provided he or they do so "within 90 days after such vacancy occurs." A quorum of the members is not required by the statute.[8]

The last sentence in the above quotation should not be overlooked. By express provision of statute, an extremely important function of the board or its members, namely, the filling of vacancies on the board, may be transacted by far less than a quorum of the board. It should be re-emphasized that this situation is made possible only by express statutory provision.

THE SCHOOL BOARD MEETING

In General

It has frequently been said that school district business can legally be transacted only at a legal meeting of the board. Although many states specify the requirements for legal board meetings, much of the litigation on the points in this section is resolved according to common law rules. Cases in which board action has been attacked upon the ground that the action was taken at an illegal board meeting are very numerous indeed. In view of this fact, it is extremely important that board members understand thoroughly the legal requirements of a legal board meeting.

Notice of Meeting

It is perhaps accurate to say that the legality of board meetings is more frequently attacked upon the ground that legally adequate notice of the meeting had not been given than upon any other single ground. Particularly in smaller districts, and in some that are not so small, there is often the tendency for members of the board to meet informally and attempt to transact school business. Often little thought is given to the legality of their meetings until a legal controversy arises. Since the requirement of notice has many aspects, we shall now give consideration to those which appear to have been litigated most frequently.

Regular Meetings. The requirement that notice of board meetings be given has different applications in regular as distinguished from special meetings. A regular meeting is one convened at a stated time and place pursuant to a general order, statute, or resolution of the board. A meeting called for a special purpose is a special meeting. Since, by hypothesis, regular meetings are held at a stated time and place, board members are expected to know of them, and no notice of regular meetings is required. This rule extends to notice of the meeting itself and to notice of the purpose of the meeting. A case which arose in Oregon will illustrate the application of the rule. It arose when four teachers had entered into teaching contracts with the school board at one of its meetings. As often happens, there was a change in the membership of the board, and the second board repudiated the contracts entered into with the teachers by the first board. In a suit brought by the teachers to recover on these contracts, the board contended that the contracts were illegal and void because the meeting at which they were authorized was not a legal meeting since notice as required by statute had not been given. The adequacy of the notice and the validity of the meeting were sustained by the Supreme Court of Oregon. Under the statute of that state, the court held that no notice of regular meetings need be given to board members.[9]

Special Meetings. It is the uniform rule that notice to board members is required for special meetings. In some states this point is covered specifically by statute. However, notice of special meetings is required to be given even if the statute does not expressly so provide. The obvious reason is that in the absence of such notice board members would not know the time or place of the meeting. The policy behind this requirement was stated by the Supreme Court of Maine in the following language:

> It is of course essential that there be some definite requirement of notice for meetings of school boards, since such a board is a deliberative body, every member of which is entitled to be present at every meeting to counsel and advise on any and every action which the committee is authorized by law to take. . . .[10]

A case decided by the Supreme Court of Wyoming illustrates the application of the rule in states which do not have statutes requiring notice of special board meetings. The controversy there arose over the refusal of the school board to reimburse the plaintiffs for room, board, and other expenses sustained by them in sending their children to elementary school in another district. The parents contended that the school board had agreed to pay each of them the sum of $45.00 per month for this purpose in lieu of maintaining a special school for their children. In support of this contention it appeared that two members of the board came together and signed a paper purporting to be the minutes of the meeting which ordered paid the amount then due, and directed that other payments be paid as they came due. All members of the board agreed that the third member had not been notified of the meeting. Although Wyoming has no statute requiring notice of special meetings of the board, the Supreme Court of that state held that the action taken by only two members of the board, the other being absent and unnotified, was their individual act and not binding upon the board or the district.[11] In states that do have statutes requiring that notice be given of a special meeting these statutes are regarded as mandatory. It is the general rule that where the charter, statute, or by-law of a corporation such as a school district provides a method by which the notice shall be given of a special meeting, the provision must be obeyed.

Time of Notice. In some states the statutes expressly specify the number of days notice board members must receive of a special board meeting. When statutes of this type appear, of course they must be obeyed. Difficulty arises, however, when it is sought to establish the length of time before a meeting that notice must be given in the absence of a statute on the point. When the matter is not controlled by statute, the courts hold that the length of time before the meeting that notice must be given must be reasonable. A Minnesota case illustrates this proposition. It involved a suit by a teacher to recover damages for breach of a contract to teach. Whether there was a valid contract depended upon whether sufficient notice of the board meeting at which the contract was entered into had been given to the chairman of the board. The only notice that he had received was given by the teacher herself just a few minutes before the meeting was to be held. Under these circumstances the chairman of the board refused to attend the meeting and the other two members proceeded to enter into a contract with the teacher. The Minnesota statute contained no provision with respect to the time notice of the meeting should be given. The highest court of that state held that the meeting was not legal because of the insufficiency of the notice. As to the time notice must be given the court said:

> There is no doubt also that the notice must be a reasonable one as to the length of time before the meeting . . . the time given was wholly unreasonable. [The chairman] . . . was hardly bound to quit the work he had started to do and rush over to attend a suddenly called meeting of the board. The notice should have given him a reasonable opportunity to attend the meeting.[12]

From the language quoted it may be inferred that the board member should have sufficient notice to enable him to attend the meeting without undue interruption of his personal affairs. Clearly, meetings may not be called suddenly.

Under certain circumstances a special meeting may be held valid despite the fact that legal notice of the meeting was not given. For example, when all members of the board attend and participate in the meeting, the meeting is legal regardless of whether the notice of the meeting was legally sufficient. In the final analysis, the only purpose of requiring notice is to enable board members to be present and participate in the meeting. If, despite the lack of notice, all members appear, the purpose of the rule requiring that notice be given has been accomplished. Indeed their presence at the meeting is proof that they had notice of it. This exception is frequently stated in terms of waiver of notice; that is, a board member may waive legal notice and attend and participate in the meeting. As a matter of procedure, however, the secretary of the board would be well advised to have on hand certain printed waiver-of-notice forms, and if special meetings are held hurriedly and before legal notice can be given, each member might be asked to sign a waiver of notice. The fact of such signing should be entered on the minutes. This procedure makes available excellent evidence of the legality of the meeting if subsequently it should be attacked because of alleged insufficiency of notice.

Another situation in which notice of meeting is not necessary is that in which the meeting has been adjourned to a later time. It should be emphasized, however, that this rule has no application unless the meeting which is adjourned was regularly called and held. An excellent illustration and statement of the rule appears in an opinion by the Court of Civil Appeals of Texas. Here, again, we find the too familiar situation in which dissension existed between two factions of the school board. One faction wished to retain the incumbent superintendent; the other group was determined to elect someone else to the position. Four members of the board met at a hastily called meeting and elected another person to the superintendency. Apparently there was some doubt in the minds of these board members as to the validity of their action. This uncertainty is evidenced by the fact that a week later they called another meeting on very short notice for the purpose of ratifying their action at the earlier meeting. Prior to this meeting feelings ran rather high and one of the board members was assaulted before the second meeting had been convened. Thereupon another board member assumed the responsibility of adjourning the meeting until 2 o'clock on the afternoon of a later day. This adjourned meeting was duly held. Later the opposing faction on the board contested the validity of the new superintendent's contract, contending that the adjourned meeting was illegal because proper notice of it had not been given to members of the board.

The court sustained the validity of the meeting despite the fact that no formal notice had been given of the adjourned meeting. The court's reasoning on the point is as follows:

It is sound reasoning to hold that special notice of an adjourned meeting is generally unnecessary where the fact and record of adjournment constitutes a notice, and these facts arose at a meeting that was regularly called. . . . But it is likewise essential to the application of such rule that the original meeting shall have been regularly notified and legally held and that its minutes show the specific time to which it is adjourned.[13]

Finally, the notice requirement does not apply when it appears that it would be futile to give notice. For example, if the officer charged with the responsibility of calling the meeting knows that a board member is ill, or unavailable for a meeting on any other ground, he need not be given notice of the meeting. The law does not require the performance of futile and useless acts. For example, in Iowa, the validity of a special meeting was sustained despite the fact that one member of the board was not notified because at the time of the meeting he would be in California and obviously not able to attend the meeting were he given notice.[14]

Form and Content of Notice. The question frequently arises whether notice of board meetings must be in writing. In some states written notice is required. If written notice is required the requirement is mandatory and must be satisfied except, of course, when all members appear and participate in the meeting despite lack of the required written notice. Upon occasion a statute on the point may be so ambiguous as to leave in doubt whether it actually requires written notice. The Iowa statute is a case in point. It requires that special meetings may be called "upon notice specifying the time and place, delivered to each member." The business transacted at a special board meeting was challenged on the ground that this statute required written notice, and such written notice had not been given to the board. The Supreme Court of Iowa sustained the validity of the notice to one board member who had been notified by telephone. In other words, the court was of the opinion that the statute did not require written notice:

> The mere fact that it must be delivered does not require . . . [that the notice be written] for notice by word of mouth may be delivered quite as effectively as one in writing. What this exacts is that it actually reach the several members, so that each shall be informed of the time and place of the meeting. . . . For this purpose, oral notice would be as effective as written, and there is nothing in the context indicating that one was intended rather than the other. If either, oral would be the more likely to be prescribed, because the more likely to be resorted to.[15]

The rule is well established that the notice of meetings must at least state the time and place of the meeting. The basis of this requirement is so obvious as to require no discussion. Certainly notice of a meeting has no legal or practical value to him who receives it unless he is also informed of the time and place of the meeting.

The courts are not in agreement about whether the notice must specify the purpose for which the meeting is called. Again, of course, if the state in which the question arises has a statute providing that the notice must also state the purpose of the meeting, that requirement must be satisfied. Missouri is among the states having such a requirement. The law there requires that each member shall have due notice of the time, place and purpose of the meeting. At the risk of being unduly repetitious, it should be stated again that if, despite the inadequacy of the notice required by law, all members of the board attend and participate in the meeting, the meeting is legally valid.

Place of Meeting

Although the problem does not seem to have reached the courts frequently, the place of a meeting of the board may be very important with respect to the validity of some action taken at the meeting. The rule seems to be that any attempted action by the school board taken at a meeting held outside the geographical limits of the district is invalid in the absence of a statute permitting meetings to be held outside the district. The point was litigated in Kansas. It appears that two districts were planning to construct a school building to be used jointly by the two districts. The construction of the building was authorized by the board at a meeting called in the office of the County Superintendent, which was outside the territorial limits of the districts. The Supreme Court of Kansas, without extended discussion, invalidated the action of the board, specifically stating that the meeting was invalid because it was held outside the district territorial limits.[16]

Perhaps the best statement of the policy requiring board meetings to be held within the district, appears in a fairly old case decided by the Appellate Court of Missouri. It involved the usual situation in which the action of the board was challenged on the ground that the board meeting was held outside the territorial limits of the district. In invalidating the board action in question, the court said:

Without any statutory enactment on the subject, it is obvious that considerations of public policy demand that the official meeings of public bodies be held within the limits of their territorial jurisdictions; otherwise, public servants might do in secret that which they would not attempt to do under public scrutiny, and thereby much injury might be done to the public welfare. It would be just as proper for the State Legislature to hold its sessions outside of the state or for a county court to meet and transact business in another county as it was for these school directors to attempt to hold a meeting outside their school district.[17]

Thus it appears that in the absence of a statute authorizing school boards to hold meetings outside the district, meetings so held are not legal.

Quorum

At this point we assume that the board meeting has been legally called and that the board is in session. Since it is frequently impossible for all board members to be present at board meetings, the question then arises as to the minimum number of members which must be present to constitute a quorum. Unless an express statute provides otherwise, the common law rule is that a majority of the authorized membership of a board constitues a quorum, and under the common law a majority of a quorum may officially transact business. In the absence of a quorum, any action taken is that of the individual members present and does not legally bind the district.

Statutes changing the common law on this point exist in several states. It is the conviction of the legislatures of these states that certain board actions are so important that they should not be permitted to be performed by a bare majority of the board. Such a statute was recently construed in Missouri. Two statutes were involved in the case. One controlled the number of board members which should constitute a quorum and the other dealt with nepotism. The statute on the quorum question is as follows:

> A majority of the board shall constitute a quorum for the transaction of business, but no contract shall be let, teacher employed, bill approved or warrant ordered unless a majority of the *whole board* [emphasis supplied] shall vote therefor.

The statute relevant to the nepotism phase of the case is as follows:

The board shall not employ one of its members as a teacher; nor shall any person be employed as a teacher who is related within the fourth degree to any board member, either by consanguinity or affinity, *where the vote of such member is necessary to the selection of such person. . . .* [Emphasis supplied.]

The case involved the legality of certain teachers' contracts. The board consisted of six members, one of whom was the husband of one of the teachers whose contracts were called into question. When the contract of the board member's wife was voted on, the board member refrained from voting, and the wife was elected by a vote of three to two. A taxpayer's suit was brought to cancel the teacher's contract on the ground that she had not been legally elected. Under the statute relating to what shall constitute a quorum in certain cases, since the teacher received the votes of only three members of a six member board, she did not receive the votes of a "majority of the whole board" and was not legally elected. Under the statute relating to nepotism, it will be observed that the wife of the board member could not have been legally elected if she had received a bare majority of the votes of the whole board, since her husband's vote was necessary to make up that majority. The St. Louis Court of Appeals cancelled the teacher's contract.[18]

There have been occasional instances of a board attempting to set its own quorum by rule or by-law. An early case which was decided in Wisconsin establishes the illegality of such practices. There, suit was brought to recover the price of installing certain equipment in school buildings. The district defended the suit on the ground that the contract was not legally voted by the board. The charter of the city provided that "all appropriations . . . for defraying current expenses shall require a two-thirds vote of all members of the board of education." It was admitted that only five of the eight board members were present and voted for awarding the contract. Of course, this is less than the required two-thirds. The board had passed a by-law to the effect that *no vote appropriating money* shall be valid unless two-thirds of all members vote their approval. The Supreme Court of Wisconsin held that the voting to approve the contract was not voting an appropriation of money, and sustained the validity of the contract. Also, it called attention to the rule that even if it had been such a vote, the contract would have been sustained as against the by-law of the board.[19] The reason is that the law prescribes the board's power, and such power cannot be enlarged, diminished, or changed by the board itself. If it could do so conceivably it might, through the passage of by-laws, completely disable itself from transacting any district business.

It is important to observe that the number necessary for a quorum of the board is not reduced when the membership of the board is not complete. A quorum will not be reduced by vacancies in the authorized membership. The operation of this rule is illustrated by a situation which reached the Court of Appeals of Kentucky. Five vacancies had occurred on a nine-member board. The court held that there was no quorum of the board. It said:

> In cities of the third class, . . . the board of education consists of nine members and a majority of said board constitutes a quorum for the transaction of business. . . . It is apparent, therefore, that five vacancies left the board without a legal quorum and disabled it from the transaction of any business.[20]

Board Meetings as Public Meetings

School board business is public business. Ordinarily, it would seem that the public should, therefore, be entitled to be present when the board is transacting its, the public's, business. Cases in this area are not numerous, although there is evidence that the problem is arising with increased frequency throughout the country. Some states, among them California, have statutes which require board meetings to be open to the public. In the absence of statute, many boards and administrators have been quite uncertain as to their obligation to admit the public and the press to board meetings. The argument of the press is the obvious one that since board business is public business, the public has a right to know what transpires at board meetings, and the press has the right and the responsibility to keep the public informed of what goes on in them.

The fact that school board meetings may be, or are, required by law to be public, does not mean that boards may not meet in executive session for a discussion of problems which are to be considered in the public meetings. The reason for this rule is obvious. In the course of carrying on district business, matters of great delicacy which must be handled by the board are bound to arise. For example, discussion of matters involving school personnel, certain matters of finance, and many others, probably should not be discussed in great detail by the board in a public meeting. In fact, if all discussions of the board were required to be carried on in a public meeting, there would seem to be little doubt that the natural reluctance by board members to discuss certain delicate matters in public, would seriously hamper free and frank discussion of such matters by the board. On the other hand, the possibility of abuses of executive sessions is manifold, and some purposes of the requirement that board meetings be public could be thwarted if the public sessions are merely to "make official" action agreed upon in executive session. The rule seems to be, therefore, that if final action on board matters is taken in an open meeting, the requirement that board meetings be public is satisfied. The Supreme Court of Utah, in a case involving the right of the public to attend board meetings and its right of access to board records, has probably expressed the rule and the reason for it as clearly as any court. It said:

> It would seem that, unless matters were of such a delicate nature or of the type where the public policy dictates non-dissemination, the meeting itself should be open to the public and press, and information concerning what transpired there should be made available at least in a general way, to both at any time thereafter by him whose duties require its recordation. There is nothing unreasonable in that under our free and democratic way of life. The truth about official acts of public servants always should be displayed in a public market place, subject to public appraisal. Any attempt to withhold information after a meeting, itself should be a subject for a wide publicity, irrespective of the fact that withholding it might prevent someone's embarrassment because of inaccuracy. . . .[21]

The conclusion here reached was in absence of a controlling statute.

A controversy involving a board of education in New Jersey is an excellent example of board procedure which the legal requirement that school board meetings be public is designed to discourage. A meeting of the board had been called for 8 P. M. for the purpose of considering the appointment of a superintendent of schools. A majority of the board caucused at 7 P. M. ostensibly to consider applicants for the superintendency. Three of the five city commissioners attended the caucus and at 7:55 P. M. signed a resolution appointing a superintendent. The same three members of the board convened the meeting at 8 P. M., the hour for which it was called. One of the board acted as temporary chairman and after very brief formal preliminaries the resolution appointing a superintendent was adopted without any discussion and over objection from the floor that the appointment was being made without its being considered as provided in the notice of the meeting. To this the temporary chairman replied: "We have met since seven o'clock in caucus and we have decided who is the superintendent, so we are presenting to you now at eight o'clock a resolution naming . . . [the person agreed on] as Superintendent of Schools."

Proceedings were brought to test the validity of the appointment. The issue finally reached the Supreme Court of New Jersey, which held the appointment invalid. It stated that there was a definite lack of exercise of discretion and that the action of the board was arbitrary. On the public meeting point the court said:

> The open meeting they held was nothing more than a sham and, . . . it ought to be dealt with "as if it had never occurred." The Legislature has unmistakably and wisely provided that meetings of boards of education shall be public . . .; if a public meeting is to have any meaning or value, final decision must be reserved until fair opportunity to be heard thereat has been afforded. This in no wise precludes advance meeting during which there is free and full discussion, wholly tentative in nature; it does, however, justly preclude private final action such as that taken by the majority in the instant matter.[22]

CITATIONS

1. People v. Green, 58 N.Y. 295 (1874).
2. Pruitt v. Glen Rose Ind. School Dist. No. 1, 84 S.W.2d 1004 (Tex. 1935).
3. Haymaker v. State, 22 N.M. 400, 163 P. 248 (1917).
4. Application of Cole, 115 N.Y.S.2d 751 (1952).
5. Prince v. Inman, 280 S.W.2d 779 (Tex. 1955).
6. Major v. Loy, 155 S.W.2d 617 (Tex. 1941).
7. Hodgkins v. Sansom, 135 S.W.2d 759 (Tex. 1939).
8. Barton v. Brafford, 264 Ky. 480, 95 S.W.2d 6 (1936).
9. Stoddard v. School Board, 140 Ore. 703, 12 P.2d 309 (1932).
10. Elsemore v. Inhabitants of Town of Hancock, 137 Me. 243, 18 A.2d 692 (1941).
11. State v. Ellis, 37 Wyo. 124, 259 P. 812 (1927).
12. Wood v. School Dist., 137 Minn. 138, 162 N.W. 1081 (1917).
13. Birdville Ind. School Dist. v. Deen, 141 S.W.2d 680 (Tex. 1940).
14. Consolidated School Dist. v. Griffin, 201 Ia. 63, 206 N.W. 86 (1925).
15. Gallagher v. School Township, 173 Ia. 610, 154 N.W. 437 (1915).

16. State v. Rural High School Dist., 169 Kan. 671, 220 P.2d 164 (1950).
17. State v. Kessler, 136 Mo. App. 236, 117 S.W. 85 (1909).
18. Irwin v. School Dist., 256 S.W.2d 290 (Mo. App. 1953).
19. Short Conrad Co. v. School Dist., 94 Wis. 535, 69 N.W. 337 (1896).
20. Glass v. City of Hopkinsville, 225 Ky. 428, 9 S.W.2d 117 (1928).
21. Conover v. Board of Education, 1 Utah 375, 267 P.2d 768 (1954).
22. Cullum v. Board of Education, 15 N.J. 285, 104 A.2d 641 (1954).

IX

SCHOOL BOARD PROCEDURE

IN GENERAL

In order to facilitate the transaction of district business at board meetings, boards should adopt rules of procedure. If the members of the board are unaccustomed to orderly procedure, being obliged to follow a definite plan may at first seem cumbersome and wasteful of time. However, when they have become accustomed to orderly procedure, it is certain to result in a major saving of time. In addition, certain procedures are sometimes required by statute, such as the manner of voting, the order of business, and others. Furthermore, regular board procedure helps the secretary of the board to make the minutes of the meetings clear and complete. The importance of complete and clear board records will be considered later in this chapter.

POWER OF BOARDS TO ADOPT RULES OF PROCEDURE

Unless the statutes provide otherwise, boards have the authority to adopt rules of procedure. If no rules are adopted the rule is that the ordinary rules of parliamentary procedure are deemed to govern board meetings. There is a substantial number of cases in which the validity of board action has been challenged on the ground that the board did not follow proper rules of procedure in taking the action in question. A fairly recent New Mexico case indicates how the problem arises. A board had attempted to discharge a teacher who was on tenure. The teacher had appealed to the state board of education, which had reversed the decision of the local board. The local board, however, refused to abide by the decision of the state board, and the teacher brought an action to require the local board to conform to the decision of the state board. One of the defenses advanced by the local board was that the action of the state board was ineffective as a decision of the board because the vote was improper. In other words, it was argued that the state board had not followed the proper procedure. The Supreme Court of New Mexico sustained the action of the state board. The court described the action of the state board and stated the rule applicable to this case as follows:

> The records show that no rules of procedure have been adopted by the State Board of Education. It further shows that this meeting, and the hearing and decision made thereon, were handled in an orderly way and in accordance with the procedure customarily used by this board. Appellants have cited no authority to sustain their position that a 3-2 vote with six members of the board present, the sixth member being elected president pro-tempore and abstaining from voting, is so improper as to negate the action of the board. In the absence of the adoption of rules on procedure and in the absence of statutory regulations, the generally accepted rules of parliamentary procedure would control.[1]

The lesson to be learned from this decision is that boards should establish and publish their rules of procedure. In some cases it may be desirable for boards to have special rules of procedure at variance with general parliamentary rules. In any event, misunderstanding and criticism will be avoided or lessened if board procedures are clearly stated and communicated to all who may have matters to bring before the board. Boards, as well as courts, may be subjected to criticism if they decide cases on procedural points rather than on the merits of the cases. Particularly is this so if boards have formulated no rules, or, having formulated them, fail to give them publicity among those whom they are most likely to affect.

A number of states expressly authorize or require boards to adopt rules and by-laws. In Kentucky, for example, a statute provides that rules and by-laws shall be adopted by the board within thirty days after organization succeeding each election. Also, it is provided that once rules and by-laws are adopted they shall not be amended, suspended, or repealed, except upon an affirmative vote of not less than two-thirds of the board members in office at the time the question arises. That great care should be exercised in the formulation and adoption of rules and by-laws is shown by a controversy involving the school board of Louisville. Among the rules and by-laws adopted by it was one to the effect that a purchase aggregating $500 might be made without advertising for bids. The implication is that any amount above this sum should be awarded to the lowest bidder. In disregard of its own rules and by-laws, the board purchased pianos from a seller for $2500 without advertising for bids. We then find the familiar situation in which the membership of the board changed and the board, as then constituted, refused to complete the purchase of the pianos. The seller sued to force the board to accept and pay for them. The action was unsuccessful. The Court of Appeals of Kentucky held that the statute mentioned above did more than give the board authority to adopt rules and by-laws; it held that the legislative intent was to give such rules and by-laws adopted by the board the effect and force of the statutory provision authorizing them. In other words, the rules and by-laws were given the effect and force of law, and, therefore, the board could not act otherwise than in compliance with them.[2]

In the states in which there are statutes of the type in effect in Kentucky, the formulation and adoption of rules and by-laws are matters of very great importance. All laws and rules, though necessarily restrictive, are designed to facilitate and not impede the work of the body operating under them. It should be noted that, generally, the more detailed rules of procedures are the more restrictive they may tend to become. When a statute renders it relatively difficult to amend rules and by-laws, perhaps it is advisable to draw them in relatively general terms. This would leave the board a measure of freedom to change the rules and by-laws to meet special conditions as they arise. Rules and by-laws should be so designed as to guide the action of the board rather than to restrict it unduly.

The type of rule and regulation which should be adopted by a particular district depends largely upon the type and amount of business coming before the board. Very simple rules doubtless would be quite adequate for a small district in which the amount of business is small. Perhaps, in such districts, the general rules of parliamentary procedure may be entirely adequate. In others, special circumstances may well dictate the desirability of a set of rules quite at variance with standard parliamentary procedure. For example, it is frequently desirable to arrange the order of business in board meetings so that routine matters are disposed of first. This clears the way for the consideration of more controversial matters which often consume so much time that if they were considered first possibly no time would be left for important routine matters.

BOARD COMMITTEES

In General

The use of board committees is often advisable in order to facilitate the transaction of business at meetings of the board. This is particularly true with respect to boards in larger communities which have a large volume of business to transact. As the volume of business of districts has increased, it has become more desirable to delegate certain types of duties to board committees. For example, it might not be feasible for the entire board to pass upon the superintendent's recommendation of teachers unless its approval is merely perfunctory and formal. Thus it is not unusual to appoint a teachers committee of the board for the purpose of giving as much consideration to matters involving teachers as the circumstances require. The same thing is applicable to numerous other phases of board business, such as supplies, buildings, transportation, curriculum, and many others. There is, of course, the danger that board committees may, in fact, pass upon matters which should have the attention of the whole board. It follows that there are limitations upon the extent to which committee recommendations should be adopted without consideration of the full board.

Simply stated, the legal rule is that the board cannot delegate to a board committee the performance of any discretionary functions, although it may delegate to the committee the performance of ministerial functions. This is another application of the familiar rule that a school board may act only as a board and at a legal board meeting. Also it cannot take legally valid action by consulting each board member individually even though each board member individually agrees and consents to the proposal presented to him. Referring again to the hypothetical teachers committee, there is no doubt that the teachers committee may interview teachers, conduct investigations into the qualifications of teachers, and make such recommendations to the whole board as it may see fit. On the other hand, it may not finally enter into a contract with the teachers since this involves a matter of discretion which cannot be delegated by the board to the committee.

A rather old case which arose in Iowa contains an excellent statement of the rule. It had been legally determined by the school board that a schoolhouse should be constructed in the district. The board delegated to a building committee the complete responsibility for implementing the board's decision to carry out the construction. However, this delegation went so far as to charge the committee of the board with the responsibility of selecting a site, adopting plans for the schoolhouse, and awarding the contract to the contractor. An action was brought to enjoin the carrying out of the contract. It was alleged that the board had no authority to delegate to the committee the functions above described. In other words, the contract was attacked on the ground that the board had delegated to the committee discretionary matters, which delegation is contrary to law. The Supreme Court of Iowa agreed with those who attacked the validity of the contract. It said:

> But the action of the board in appointing a committee to select and procure the site for the new schoolhouse, in adopting the plans for the schoolhouse, and in attempting to award the contract for the construction thereof, were illegal and without authority of law, and defendants should have been enjoined from entering into the contract for the erection of the schoolhouse at the place selected by them, or at any other place not selected by the school board, and from in any manner, as a committee, participating in the making of a contract for the erection of the schoolhouse.[3]

There probably would have been no question as to the legality of the action of the committee if it had restricted its actions to investigating available school sites, surveying school plans, making recommendations to the board as to the plans it considered desirable, and suggesting to the board terms of the proposed contract with the contractors. There would appear to be little or no doubt that the actual signing of the contract might be delegated by the board to others when the final terms of the contract actually have been settled by the whole board. The physical act of signing doubtless would be considered a ministerial as distinguished from a discretionary act, and thus could be delegated.

In North Carolina a full board attempted to delegate to its property committee the authority to sell certain district property. This committee, through its chairman, entered into a contract in behalf of the district to sell the property to a particular buyer. Another buyer who indicated a willingness to pay a higher price than the amount specified in the agreement of the committee to sell, attacked the contract on the ground that the sale of district property involved the exercise of discretion which could not be delegated to a committee. The Supreme Court of North

Carolina agreed that this was a non-delegable function of the board. The holding and the philosophy of the court is indicated in the following language:

> This is an allegation and admission that the Trustees attempted to delegate a non-delegable power and responsibility. It means that they attempted to abdicate their solemn trust by a delegation of their authority. "The principle is a plain one that the public powers or trusts devolved by law or charter upon the council or governing body, to be exercised by it when and in such manner as it shall deem best, cannot be delegated to others. This principle may not prevent the delegation of duties which are ministerial, but where the trust committed to the governing body involves the exercise of functions which partake of a judicial character, it may not be delegated."[4]

Disbursement of School Funds by Board Committees

Among the non-delegable duties of the board is the disbursement of school funds. Clearly, determination of how school funds shall be spent is a matter involving discretion which must be exercised by the whole board and not by a committee of it. Of course, the finance committee may have delegated to it the responsibility of preparing and scrutinizing the proposed school budget and the making of recommendations to the whole board with reference to it.

There have been a few instances in which the question has arisen as to whether particular funds in the board's possession and control were public funds. The problem seems to have been considered more often in Pennsylvania than elsewhere; hence two cases from that state will serve to illustrate the problem involved. In the first case to be considered, the question arose as to the right of the auditor to audit certain funds which had been expended by the board. Here all activity funds, such as those for athletics, publications, dramatics, the school annual, and numerous other activities, were, by board resolution, consolidated under the supervision of the supervising principal and the control of the school board. The Pennsylvania law requires that funds belonging to or controlled by the district shall be properly audited. The question then arose whether activity funds were funds "belonging to or controlled by the district." Extracurricular funds were, according to the Supreme Court of Pennsylvania, public funds and as such subject to audit. It said:

. . . it is certainly true that, if a school operates and expends tax money for the acquisition, maintenance and lighting of the playing field, or for the payment of the services of a coach, the admissions charged result from the use of public property of the school district, must go into the official account of the treasurer thereof, and are subject to audit.[5]

It is very important, according to the court, to determine the source of funds in order to establish whether they are public. If they are produced by public facilities and employees, they are certainly public in nature.

The delegation of control of funds so produced, as well as others, has been attempted by boards. "Incidental" funds have been established, and board committees or school employees have been authorized to expend them. Unfortunately, the case which contains the best treatment of this specific problem did not reach the highest court of the state in which it arose, namely, Pennsylvania. It involved an attempt to remove certain board members from office because of their alleged misconduct in disbursement of school funds. Members of the board proceeded upon the assumption that athletic activities, high school band organizations, and other extracurricular activities may be entirely segregated from the supervision and control of the board. They contended that they might delegate to an appointed athletic board of control all jurisdiction over these activities, including the handling of the finances incident to the management of the activities. They insisted that the purchase of team equipment, the purchase of new uniforms for the band, and the expenditure of proceeds arising from these activities, were matters for the sole determination of the athletic board; that the board as a whole was under no legal obligation to supervise the conduct of the athletic board. Proceeding from this theory, the athletic board deposited the proceeds of the athletic games in a bank, not an approved depositary, and checked them out in payment of bills for athletic equipment and band uniforms. It made no attempt to comply with the law as to the manner of authorizing and making payment by school boards. Indeed, the game proceeds were never deposited in the school treasury. Apparently this procedure was not questioned until the full board drew a voucher for over $900 to pay for equipment which the athletic board had purchased. The athletic board had exhausted the funds which had been received as income from athletic games, and the full board sought to assume the deficit and pay for the equipment.

The court refused to remove the board members since it held that their conduct was the result of an "error in judgment." However, it condemned the procedure in no uncertain terms. Concerning the status of the proceeds of activities and the manner of handling them by the board, the court said:

> The proceeds of these activities belong to the board of school directors and must be accounted for in the same manner that other funds of the school district are accounted for. . . .

> The school board may hereafter continue to permit the athletic board of control to manage and direct extra-curricular activities, but all monies received therefrom and all expenditures for equipment to be used therein, must be reported to and approved by the board of directors as a board. The board of athletic control must be considered merely as a committee, with like powers and duties as a teachers' committee, the committee on supplies, or the building committee.[6]

These two cases sustained the proposition that proceeds from school activities are public funds, just as are tax funds. Thus, their expenditure may not be delegated to a committee of the board or to the superintendent, supervising principal, or any other school employees, and they are subject to audit as school funds.

BOARD VOTING

In the absence of statute to the contrary, voting by board members may be by any of the usual methods, such as orally, by raising of hands, or by secret ballot. Unless the statute dictates a different method, the board may establish its own voting procedure. Furthermore, it may legally decide to follow one procedure on a particular issue and an entirely different procedure on others. For example, it may decide to vote orally on one issue and take a secret ballot on another issue, even though both these issues may be before the board in the same meeting.

Of course, if there is a statute that requires a voice or a roll-call vote on a particular matter the statute is mandatory. That is, the statute must be complied with or the action taken by the board on the question upon which the vote was taken will be held invalid. Illinois, for example, has a statute providing that a yea-and-nay vote on all questions involving the expenditure of money should be taken. In a case involving the statute the school board had employed a teacher without complying with the requirements of the statute as to the manner of voting. The teacher accepted employment under this vote, but a few days later the board rescinded its action and declined to abide by its agreement with the teacher. The Appellate Court of Illinois held that the action of the board was invalid, and refused to permit the teacher to recover damages in her suit against the board on her alleged contract. The purpose of the statute is described by the court as follows:

> The purpose of the statute in requiring a yea and nay vote and the recording of the same is to give the tax payers an opportunity to know how each member voted. The method followed by . . . [the board] gives no such information and is in direct violation of the statutory provisions. The verbal acceptance of employment by . . . [the teacher] did not operate as a waiver of the statutory requirements for they were enacted for the benefit of the taxpayers of the district and no liability could be created against the district except by a compliance therewith.[7]

A member of the board who is present at a meeting at which there is a quorum sufficient for the purpose of transacting business, has a duty to vote on matters that come before the board. If he refrains from voting on any matter he will be regarded as acquiescing in rather than opposing the motion before the board. It is sometimes stated that he will be regarded as voting with the majority. Of course, the only situation in which there will be any difference between the two applications of the rule would occur when the other members of the board who do vote are evenly divided on the motion. Under such circumstances, it is probably safe to assume that the court would then hold that the non-voting member supported rather than opposed the motion. From this rule it is to be observed that a board member may not escape his duty and responsibility to vote merely by refraining from casting his vote. Of course, it is probably possible for a board member to escape his responsibility by absenting himself from the meeting. As far as we are aware, it has never been judicially stated that a board member will be held to have voted with the majority or voted in favor of a motion if he is not present at the meeting. As a matter of principle, a board member should express himself on motions before the board or resign his position. There certainly is an implied agreement on the part of a board member, when he accepts a position on the board, that he will exercise his judgment on school matters.

The Kansas City, Missouri, Court of Appeals applied the rule in a typical case. The case involved the legality of a meeting at which an election pertaining to consolidation of school districts had been called. Two members of a three-member board attended the meeting. The third member declined to attend, stating that he was opposed to calling the election. The president of the board, who was in favor of calling the election, presented the petition to the other member who was present, but the latter refused to vote for or against the proposition. The president, however, issued the call for the election. Certain individuals contested the validity of the election called. They contended that the action taken was that of the board president, and not that of the board. The court held that the election was legally called, despite the fact that only one member, the president of the board, actually voted to call it. The court said:

> There were two of the three members of the School Board present and by their presence constituted a quorum for the transaction of business, and it became and was the duty of each member to vote for or against any proposition which was presented to them. . . . [The president] voted in favor of submitting the question of annexation and . . . [the other member present] did not vote. His reasons for not voting are of no consequence because, as stated above, it was his duty to vote for or against the question submitted. In . . . [another case] we held that when a member of a school board sits silently by when given an opportunity to vote, he is regarded as acquiescing in, rather than opposing, the measure, and is regarded in law as voting with the majority. . . .[8]

Difficulty has arisen concerning the right or the responsibility of the chairman or the presiding officer of the school board to cast his vote. His right or responsibility to vote is not limited to the familiar situation in which the other members of the board are evenly divided on the matter before them. It has been held that in cases where his vote would establish a majority required by law, the chairman will be deemed to have voted in favor of the motion by the act of declaring that the motion has passed. This question arose in Idaho. It involved an action brought to enjoin the issuance and sale of bonds that had been authorized at a school district bond election. One of the grounds relied upon was that the submission of the question to the electors was not approved by a majority of the board as was required by the Idaho law. There were five members on the board. Only four of them were in attendance at the meeting at which the question of the submission of the bond issue to the electors was under consideration. Of the four members present two voted in favor of the resolution and one voted against it, with the chairman not voting. The board pleaded that the chairman had approved and favored the bond issue and had so expressed himself on numerous occasions. It also alleged that he had expressed himself as favoring the motion on the night of the meeting, but that he had refrained from voting because he felt that as chairman he should not vote, since a majority of the trustees present had voted in favor of the motion. As against the contention that the measure had not been approved by the required majority, the court said:

> The approval of the chairman of the board of trustees, while irregular, is sufficiently indicated by the admitted facts to constitute a sufficient compliance with . . . [the Idaho law].[9]

It is to be observed that this case is not one in which a board member is held to have voted affirmatively on a proposition by virtue of remaining silent when the vote is taken. Rather the case is authority for the proposition that a chairman is held to have cast the decisive affirmative vote when he declares that the motion has passed.

BOARD HEARINGS

When Required

It is basic in the philosophy of the American law that an individual shall not be condemned, or other legal action taken against him, without his being afforded the opportunity of being heard in his own behalf. This right to a hearing is a very important one which the courts zealously protect. However, the right to a hearing does not exist in all school controversies. In most states, for example, temporary teachers may be discharged without a hearing. In others a hearing is required before even a temporary teacher may be discharged. Other aspects of dismissal procedure are considered in Chapter IV.

The hearing problem most frequently arises under tenure statutes providing that tenure teachers may be discharged only for cause. However, it may arise also in related problems such as promotion and transfer, and frequently arises in cases of non-tenure teachers when an attempt is made to discharge them for cause before the termination of their contract. The problem also has arisen in cases involving the removal of school officials from office and in other school matters.

Clearly, if a statute expressly provides, as many tenure statutes do, that a hearing shall be required, legal action can be taken only after a hearing. However, the duty to hold a hearing also arises by implication when a statute provides that certain action can be taken only for cause, the inference being that cause can be established only after a hearing. The latter question arose in North Carolina. A county board of education had elected a member to a two-year term on a school committee in a district where school committees are elected by the county board of education. Before the expiration of his term the board of education entered an order removing him from office under the provisions of a statute which did not expressly require a hearing but which did provide that removal of a member of the school committee was legally possible only on specified statutory grounds. In holding that a hearing was necessary, even though the statute did not expressly require it, the Supreme Court of North Carolina said:

> The law clearly contemplates that any school committeeman against whom the statutory proceeding for removal is brought shall be given notice of the proceeding, and of the charges against him, and afforded an opportunity to be heard and to produce testimony in his defense, and that the county board of education shall not remove him from his office unless it determines after a full fair hearing on the merits that one or more of the specified causes for removal has been established by the evidence.[10]

Whether a hearing would be required in the absence of an express provision when a teacher is discharged was considered by the Supreme Court of Montana in a case where the court divided three to two on the decision, with four of the five judges writing separate opinions. The teacher, it appears, had taught in Montana schools for seventeen years and had a continuing contract when she was discharged without the filing of charges and without a hearing. The majority of the court based its decision that no hearing was required on the fact that the law made no explicit provision for any showing of cause, or for a hearing before a teacher could be discharged.[11]

Obviously a hearing may not be required in many situations even though it may involve board action affecting individual teachers. There is a broad area of board discretion which may be exercised solely on the judgment of the board without the necessity of a hearing, and without the board's being obliged to explain the action taken. Such matters as teacher rating, the assignment of teachers, and certain salary considerations doubtless would fall within this area. An "unsatisfactory rating" case which arose in Pennsylvania will illustrate the judicial attitude in such matters. The teacher involved sought to have her temporary status raised to permanent tenure status. Although the Pennsylvania statute did not require that the teacher be accorded a hearing under these circumstances, the teacher insisted that failure to grant her a hearing violated the due process of law requirement. The Supreme Court of Pennsylvania, in holding that the teacher was not entitled to a hearing under these circumstances, said:

> There was no provision in the statute authorizing or providing for a hearing for a temporary teacher *who desired to attain permanent status,* and in the absence thereof, plaintiff had no property or other vested right in or to the position or status of a permanent teacher.[12]

In other words, teacher competence, relative standing of teachers in their positions, and possibly other similar matters need not be the subject of a hearing as a condition precedent to the board taking a valid action on them. From the cases it can be gathered that distinguishing between situations in which a hearing must be had and those in which it is not required may sometimes be a problem of considerable nicety.

In at least one state, namely, Ohio, it has been judicially determined that an unsuccessful bidder, under a competitive bid statute, is not entitled to a hearing to determine whether the bidder is in fact "responsible." In the case in point it appeared that the board had determined that a certain bidder was not responsible although his bid was the lowest. The board had dealt with this bidder upon other occasions and had found that his work was not entirely satisfactory. For this reason his bid was rejected and the contract was awarded to a higher bidder. The unsuccessful bidder then insisted that the board was in no position to determine legally that he was not responsible without affording the bidder a hearing at which he would be permitted to produce evidence of his responsibility. The court held that the unsuccessful bidder had no right to such a hearing.[13] A different rule obtains in a few states, among them the state of New Jersey, in which unsuccessful bidders are entitled to a hearing as to why they were unsuccessful.

It should be noted here that hearings are frequently required by statute on budgets, proposed bond issues, district reorganizations, and other such matters. In such cases, the applicable statute should be followed strictly. Hearings are deemed to be integral parts of the statutory procedure. Obviously, in this type of hearing there would be no requirements such as the filing of charges and the giving of notice to individuals.

Procedure in School Board Hearings

In some states the procedure to be followed in board hearings is described in the law in considerable detail. Some of the common requirements are that written charges be filed, that notice of the charges and the hearing must be presented to the person charged, that he must have the opportunity to present evidence, that the right to cross-examine witnesses must be given, that legal counsel must be permitted if the person charged desires it, and that the testimony taken normally should be under oath. However, more often statutes only require that a hearing be held, without specifying the procedure to be followed. The Supreme Court of Alabama has outlined generally the accepted requirements with respect to a hearing in the absence of a controlling statutory provision as follows:

> No particular form of procedure is prescribed for hearings under the statutes herein requested, but of course due process must be observed. . . . The Teacher Tenure Law in its provisions clearly contemplates the rudimentary requirements of fair play with reasonable notice and opportunity to be present, information as to charges made and opportunity to controvert such charges, the right to examine and cross-examine witnesses and submit evidence and to be heard in person or by counsel.[14]

From this statement of the usual hearing requirements it will be observed that hearings before boards need not be conducted in accordance with the strict rules prevailing in court proceedings. Formal rules of evidence and the usual formalities of a trial need not be followed. If boards were required to adhere to strict court procedure in their hearings, it would be impossible, in most cases, for the board to discharge its hearing responsibility. Boards are not constituted of lawyers, and very frequently no member of the board is a lawyer. Under such informal proceedings, the board may conduct the hearing and judge the merits of the case despite the fact that it also may be the agency preferring the charges. If final decision on the matter is withheld until those accused have been given notice and an opportunity to be heard, board members are not disqualified from hearing and finally determining the issues involved.

Courts uniformly agree that the right to a hearing includes the right to be represented by legal counsel. A representative case on this point arose in West Virginia. It appears that a superintendent of schools had been discharged by the board of education on various charges, which charges were written and filed in accordance with the provisions of the statute. A hearing was held at which the superintendent was not permitted to be represented by counsel and witnesses testified without being sworn. The court did not hesitate to find that under these circumstances the superintendent was denied the hearing contemplated by the statutes. With reference to the failure to permit the superintendent to be represented by counsel the court stated:

> The superintendent, who was to enter upon a hearing by which his right to an important and profitable office for a definite term of years should be determined, was denied the assistance of legal counsel. We unhesitatingly say that this was the deprivation of a hearing as contemplated by statute. . . . In America, the very word "hearing", both in common and legal parlance, implies some kind of trial, formal or informal, and presupposes permission to have legal aid if desired.[15]

The court also stated that the fact that no witnesses were sworn would alone nullify the hearing. It expressed the opinion that the hearing by any tribunal contemplates the taking of evidence, and that oral testimony presupposes the administration of an oath.

While most courts would agree with the West Virginia court that the right to a hearing carries the right to be represented by counsel, some courts have held that witnesses in a hearing need not be sworn. This question arose in Colorado. A teacher had been dismissed because of general incompetency prior to the termination of her contract, and contended that she had been denied "due process" despite the fact that a hearing had been held, charges had been filed, she had been represented by counsel, and witnesses had been examined and cross-examined. However, all testimony had been taken without oath or affirmation. The Supreme Court of Colorado held that the informality of board hearings extends even to the point of not requiring that testimony be taken under oath.[16] The same conclusion was reached by the Supreme Court of Arizona. This court said:

The law does not make any provision for trial before the board but leaves it entirely with that body to adopt the procedural rules that will safeguard and protect the rights of all parties. The board may accept, as it did in this case, information bearing upon the issue before it, whether obtained under oath of the informant or not. It is not supposed to adhere to the strict rules of evidence ordinarily observed in courts.[17]

The board may, because of statute or otherwise, be required to make express findings of fact indicating the evidence relied on in reaching its findings. For example, in Florida a school principal had been removed for cause under the tenure laws of that state. The statute specified in some detail the procedure to be followed. The principal had been charged with certain immoral conduct and the board, after a hearing, found him guilty and ordered his dismissal. The case finally reached the Supreme Court of Florida. The statute merely provided that the board before discharging an accused teacher must find that one or more of the charges which are the legal bases upon which a teacher may be discharged have been established. The court interpreted this provision to require the board to set out the facts which it found were established by the evidence so that the court could determine whether the facts as found by the board constituted legal grounds for removal, and whether the evidence supported the finding. The reason for the rule, according to the court, is that unless the facts are set out the reviewing court would be compelled to grope in the dark or resort to guesswork as to what facts the board had found to be true and what facts alleged were not found to be true.[18] The case was sent back to the board for specific findings of facts by it. Under these circumstances, it is good procedure in all cases to set out in considerable detail in the board's record of the hearing a clear statement of the facts which the board had concluded the evidence established. Of course, it would be desirable to have a legal stenographer record the entire proceedings.

The Correction of Irregular Board Hearings

Legality of hearings has frequently been challenged on the ground that boards failed to adhere strictly to statutory procedure. When challenges arise, boards may elect to stand upon their decisions regardless of the irregular procedure, or they may attempt to regularize them by subsequent action. Earlier in this work it was pointed out that a contract the validity of which might be questioned because of some illegal procedure may subsequently be ratified by board action. The possible regularization of irregular board hearings is closely related to the contractual ratification matter.

An excellent illustration of an attempted regularization of a defective hearing has been passed upon by the Supreme Court of New Jersey. The business manager of a board of education had been discharged from his position. Lengthy hearings had been held on charges against him after a committee of three members of the board, following an investigation, had recommended discharging him. The full board consisted of nine members. The hearing extended over several weeks. On the several dates on which the hearings were held, one or two members of the board were absent. At the conclusion of the hearing only two members had heard all of the testimony presented. The attorney for the manager insisted that since only two members of the board had heard the testimony it was legally unable to render a decision in the matter. The board then voted to strike from the record and withdraw from consideration testimony which had not been heard by a majority of the board. Then, in order to regularize the proceedings, the board resolved to recall those witnesses who had not been heard by the entire board. About two months after the conclusion of the first hearing, the board reconvened with eight of the nine board members present. Over the manager's objections, the recalled witnesses were heard, all the evidence was then considered, and the resolution of dismissal was then passed.

It was the manager's contention that it was improper for the board to reopen the case and rehear testimony of witnesses after the case had been closed. The court overruled this contention and sustained the action of the board in regularizing the proceedings. The court said:

> We know of no vested right in a defendant to prevent a reopening of a case or a hearing for the taking of evidence. The board realized it had made a mistake in not insisting that all its members or a quorum thereof hear all the evidence, and in our judgment it took the only proper course when it ordered that the testimony be repeated for the benefit of those who were absent.[19]

Not only in board hearings, and other similar proceedings, but in judicial proceedings as well, the courts are usually as liberal as circumstances permit in allowing the reopening of cases in order to hear additional evidence or to correct errors. In the final analysis, the purpose of such proceedings is to elicit as complete and reliable evidence as possible in order that the proper decision may be reached. In the New Jersey case, the alternative to the action taken by the board regularizing its proceedings would have been to rehear all the evidence and testimony in the case from the beginning. Such a waste of time and effort by the board will not be insisted upon by the courts unless the interest of justice and fairness clearly demands it.

Fairness and Impartiality of Board Hearings

It is axiomatic that legal hearings must be fair and impartial. If they are otherwise, they serve merely to compound injustice rather than to promote justice. Partiality and unfairness may run the entire gamut of human perversity. It may consist of hostility to the subject of a hearing, a failure or refusal to call witnesses, basing decisions on rumor and gossip rather than the sworn testimony of witnesses, the use of unfair tactics at the hearing, and the like.

A rather unusual case involving alleged partiality and unfairness, in a hearing involving a teacher, recently arose in Michigan. A teacher had been discharged and this action of the board had been appealed to the tenure commission. In the hearing before the commission the teacher introduced evidence relating to the size of the room in which the board hearing in this case had been held. The commission reversed the action of the board and ordered the teacher reinstated. The evidence showed that the teacher had advised the board of education that his witnesses and friends who would attend the meeting would number about one hundred, and he requested that adequate facilities be provided for the hearing. There was abundant evidence that the facilities were inadequate. Throughout the hearing the attitude of the board appeared to be hostile to the hearing and possibly even to the requirement that a hearing be held. Apparently it "packed" the hearing room with its own friends and witnesses, and excluded those of the teacher. The situation is described by the Supreme Court of Michigan as follows:

> There is evidence from which it can be found that prior to the first hearing the school board was notified that . . . [the teacher] would have approximately one hundred friends and witnesses present when the hearing was had; that on the night in question the hearing was held in a room approximately 12 x 24 feet; that only friends and witnesses of the school board were allowed in the room, with the exception of . . .

[the teacher] and his wife, his attorney and one witness; that from 75 to 100 people were kept out of the room by two armed policemen; that requests were made to adjourn the meeting to the library in the same school where adequate seating facilities could be had for all interested parties, but this request was refused by the school board.[20]

Under these circumstances the court invalidated the teacher dismissal hearing on the ground that hearing facilities had been inadequate.

By way of contrast we find a board of education in Connecticut exercising extreme care in its effort to conduct a fair and impartial hearing involving the discharge of a teacher. The factual situation is the familiar one of a teacher whose services were not satisfactory and whose contract the board had terminated. A hearing was requested by the teacher, and the hearing consumed five days and 1,250 pages of transcript. The teacher was discharged and he appealed his case to the court. He alleged that the action of the board was "illegal, arbitrary, discriminatory, and in abuse of its discretion."

The action of the board was sustained. The good faith and fair dealing of the board is indicated by the following language of the court:

> The test of the action of the board is whether the plaintiff had a reasonable opportunity to hear and be heard upon the charges preferred against him and whether the proceedings were conducted in a fair and impartial manner. . . . Hearings were held for five days. . . . Early in the hearing . . . [the teacher] was given an opportunity to examine the board's records, minutes and files. The hearing was postponed to enable him to prepare his case. Witnesses were summoned at his request, and those called from among persons employed by the board were publicly advised that there would be no reprisals for giving testimony in his behalf. An examination of the transcript of the proceedings demonstrates that . . . [the teacher] had a full and fair opportunity of learning what evidence there was against him and of presenting evidence in his own behalf.[21]

SCHOOL ELECTIONS

In General

A very important responsibility of school boards is that of calling and conducting school elections. Election procedure is always statutory and should be followed strictly. In fact, it has frequently been stated that the statutory procedure is mandatory and that failure to follow it will invalidate the election. However, there are a very large number of situations in which the legality of school elections has been sustained despite the failure of boards to follow the letter of the statutory election procedure. This should not encourage carelessness in school elections, however. It is particularly important that the letter of the law be followed when the election in question involves a bond issue or other important financial matters. Prospective purchasers of bonds usually require the approval of attorneys specializing in such matters, as a condition to the purchase of the bonds. These attorneys check with great care the procedure of the board in calling the bond election. Since their professional reputation is involved, they are sometimes inclined to disapprove a bond issue if there are errors in the election procedures even if the error is so slight as to be disregarded by a court. Failure to follow strictly the statutory election requirements may, at least, delay the issuance of the bonds involved. In the discussion which follows consideration will be given to the legal consequences of mistakes or irregularities in the calling and conducting of school elections.

Signatures on Petitions

In most states elections on the annexation of territory, district reorganizations, bond issues, and certain other matters are initiated by petitions signed by a number of voters as required by statute. The officials, often the board of education, who must pass on these petitions have a heavy burden, for they must determine whether the signers are in fact legal electors, and whether the signatures are genuine. If they are found to be genuine the officials are bound to call the elections when the petition, in apparent good form, is presented to it. A case which recently arose in Oklahoma illustrates the nature of the problem. In that state the statutes did not expressly give the official any power to review the petition, but the highest court of that state held that he must examine the petition and determine that it is sufficient before he calls the election. Of course, the same would be true if, instead of requiring a particular official to pass upon the petition, the law places that responsibility upon the school board. This petition involved a change of boundaries of a school district. Concerning the official's responsibility, the court said:

> We think it clear that when a petition changing the boundaries of a school district is presented to the County Superintendent that the duty

rests on him to examine the petition carefully and determine whether it contains the real signatures of a majority of the qualified electors in the area affected. If it does not he has no authority to call an election. If he finds that it does contain the proper number of genuine signatures, it is clearly his duty to call the election.[22]

In this case the petition failed because the evidence showed that in many instances persons had signed names in addition to their own, husbands often signing for wives and vice versa, for example.

Although this burden upon the official or the board to determine the validity of the petitions is a heavy one, the courts do not make it unduly difficult. In some states the responsible officials or boards may rely upon the affidavits of those who circulated the petitions that the signatures are genuine and that the persons signing are electors. Furthermore, a district is saved from having its election upset if the validity of the signatures on the petition is not attacked before the election is held or before a petition has been accepted and acted upon by the responsible board or official. In other words, those who attack the validity of a petition must act promptly.

Errors in Election Notice

Inherent in the legal requirements that notice of elections be given, is the necessity of including in the notices sufficient information to inform the electors of the issues to be voted upon. There is no yardstick by means of which the exact information which must be included in election notices in all cases may be ascertained, since the amount and nature of the information required differs from case to case. In a case which arose in North Dakota involving the reorganization of school districts, the supreme court of that state expressed very well the attitude of the courts on the effect upon the election of errors in the notice of the election. The sufficiency of the notice was attacked upon the ground that it did not include a description of a part of the area involved. The court said:

> There is no charge that there was any fraud or any irregularity in the conduct of the election itself, nor that a fair and public expression of the public will was prevented by reason of anything that was done or omitted. . . . Irregularities which do not deprive any voter of a fair chance to register his will, or which do not prevent the will of the voters

from being fairly and truly ascertained and declared, do not vitiate a school election to determine the question of consolidation.[28]

It will be observed that the court was concerned much more with the effect of the erroneous election notice than it was with the fact that an error in notice had occurred. Elections are not lightly set aside by the courts. Many actions are taken in reliance upon them; school buildings are constructed; bonds are issued; contracts are entered into. The courts, knowing they cannot set back the clock and undo many and important acts which have been performed upon the assumption that the election was valid, will not declare an election invalid for the failure to dot an *i* or cross a *t*.

The Requirement That Election Notices Be Posted

One device under the law for notifying electors of an ensuing election is that of posting election notices. The statutes usually require that such notices be posted a stated number of days prior to the holding of the election, and that notices be posted in a stipulated number of "public places." The term "public place" is a relative term. A place may be a public place under one set of circumstances and might not be so considered under others. Also, under still other circumstances, a place which is relatively isolated may be considered a public place for the purpose of posting notices of elections.

The manner in which the courts deal with this problem is well illustrated by two cases which arose recently in Missouri. The first involved an election to vote on a proposed change of district boundaries. Under the law of Missouri, notices of elections on boundary changes are required to be posted in five public places in the district. The legality of the election was attacked on the ground that this requirement had not been fulfilled. It appeared that three of the five notices required were posted inside private business houses: one in the window of a drug store, one in a grocery store, and a third in a cotton gin. The question then is whether posting the notices in private business establishments is posting in "public places." The court held that this posting was in substantial compliance with the law. It was of the opinion that the posting of the three notices in question fulfilled the purpose of the statute in giving the publicity required by the nature of a notice. It stated that the notices in the places indicated would be likely to attract general attention so that the contents of the notice might reasonably be expected to become widely known and discussed in the vicinity. In describing what constitutes a public place the court quoted the following language from *Corpus Juris Secundum,* a standard legal work:

> "The term 'public place' within the meaning of a statute providing for the posting of a notice therein is relative. There are certain places which prima facie may be regarded as public places for the posting of notice, so that the party claiming otherwise must show the ground of his objection, as, for example, houses of worship, inns, and post offices. It seems that, in the absence of any place more public, a dwelling house in a sparsely inhabited community might be deemed to be a public place for the posting of notice." [24]

The second Missouri case involved a contest over the legality of a bond issue on the ground that the notices of the election had not been posted in "public places." The district was approximately ten or twelve miles square and sparsely populated. It was contended that all the notices were posted in places beside the highways in such positions that they could not be read by persons while driving by in their automobiles, or even while standing on the road. The objectors pointed out that there were many places in which the notices might have been posted where they would have been likely to be seen by more people. The Supreme Court of Missouri sustained the legality of the posting. It stated that the notice-posting statutory requirement had been satisfied if the posting was in places which gave the publicity contemplated by the nature of the notice required.[25] A tree or telephone pole may or may not be in a public place depending upon the location and circumstances. It is quite possible that had the notices been posted on the side of a telephone pole not facing the road, the holding would have been different. Certainly, "hiding" the notices would not be judicially countenanced. Good faith is an absolute requisite in such cases.

Defective Newspaper Notice of Elections

A second means of providing that notice of elections frequently required by statute is publishing a notice in newspapers. The statute in Ohio is a fairly typical one on this point. It provides that election notices shall be published in certain newspapers once a week for four consecutive weeks prior to the election. This statute was construed in a case in which the validity of a school bond election had been attacked on the ground that the newspaper publication requirement had not been satisfied. In bond elections, the notices were required to state the amount of the proposed bond issue, the purpose of the issue, the maximum term of the bonds, and the estimated additional tax rate, expressed in dollars and cents for each one hundred dollars of valuation as well as in mills for each dollar of valuation. It was conceded that the election notice had been published for the time required by law. Through error, the notice failed to state properly the amount of the annual tax levy and omitted to state in full the purpose of the issue. Also the amount of the annual tax levy in cents for each $100 of valuation was stated as being 3.2 instead of .32, the proper rate. Despite these errors, the bond issue was approved by a large majority. The legality of the election was attacked upon the ground that the errors enumerated above invalidated it. There was very substantial evidence that the election had wide publicity. Numerous articles describing the needs of the schools, the amount of the bond issue, and the uses to which the proceeds would be put appeared in several issues of the local newspapers. The Court of Appeals of Ohio sustained the validity of the bond election despite the errors in the election notice. The court applied the familiar rule that elections will not be set aside because unsubstantial errors were made in the election notices. In the final analysis, the purpose of the election notices is to provide essential information to the voters in order that they may be informed of the nature of the proposition to be voted upon. If it appears that the electors receive such information, the courts are disinclined to invalidate the election because of defective notice. The court quoted, with approval, the following language from an earlier Ohio case:

> "It had been generally held that defects, variances and irregularities in the several steps relating to the issuance of bonds should be material, harmful or both before the proceeding may be successfully attacked. . . . It has also been held that unsubstantial irregularities in . . . inaugurating an election on a bond issue which does not prejudice anyone will be disregarded, especially where the proposed bond issue as submitted was approved by considerably more than the requisite number of electors."[26]

It could hardly be plausibly argued that the errors in the Ohio case were "unsubstantial." Despite the fairly substantial irregularities which appeared in the notice, however, there was no evidence that any voter was prejudiced thereby. Apparently the voters understood thoroughly all the issues involved, or, at least, were sufficiently informed of the details of the proposition to be voted upon to be able to cast what they considered an intelligent ballot.

It should be noted in this connection that the rule referred to is applicable only in cases in which defective notice has been given. It has no application if no notice at all has been given. The reason for the distinction is that if no notice has been given the electors may have no opportunity to acquaint themselves with the issues involved. However, if some notice is given, even though it be defective, electors at least know that an election is in prospect. If they are sufficiently interested they may then inform themselves, through inquiry, of the purpose and procedure of the election.

BUDGETARY PROCEDURE

The statutory procedures for the preparation and adoption of school budgets vary greatly from state to state. However, such statutes commonly require that there be a preparation of the budget and a hearing thereon and that the budget be sufficiently itemized to enable interested persons to determine with a fair degree of accuracy the purposes for which school funds are to be expended. Also, often, there are prescriptions related to the extent to which transfers of funds may be made among the various items of the budget after it has finally been approved and adopted by the school board.

It has been observed that school board hearings need not be formal in nature and that they need not adhere to the strict procedures followed in court proceedings. The same rule is applicable to budgetary hearings. If the hearings are fair and impartial, and interested persons are afforded adequate opportunity to present to the hearing agency any objections or suggested changes in the budget, there would appear to be little doubt that the hearing would be sustained as legally valid.

The degree of particularity with which the school budget must be prepared, that is, the extent of itemization required, has been frequently litigated. Two extremes are possible on this question. The first extreme would be a very broad statement of budgetary items such as administration, instruction, capital outlay, and other broad classifications. Obviously interested parties would gain very little information from such a broad classification, and doubtless it would be judicially condemned. The other extreme would be itemization in very great detail, that is, listing expenditures for chalk, brooms, floor oil, supplies for the superintendent's office, and other such specific items. This degree of detail is not legally required. The proper extent of itemization lies somewhere between these extremes. The principle underlying the itemization requirement is well stated by the Supreme Court of Illinois as follows:

> The right of a tax payer to have stated separately what are the purposes for which public money is appropriated is firmly established, and a levy not sufficiently definite to apprise him of the purpose for which the money is to be expended is invalid. . . . His right . . . is a substantial right of which he may not be deprived. . . . On the other hand, it is equally settled that each particular item or expense for which a levy is made is not required.[27]

An important case which arose in Utah will illustrate the nature of the legal problems which arise in the area of itemization. The validity of the budget of the board of education of Salt Lake City was attacked on the ground that the board had not complied with the statute requiring itemization. The contested budget, as prepared and published, consisted of ten classifications of accounts, among them administration, operating of buildings, interest fund, building fund, and instruction. Each of these classifications had been broken down, and the completed budget showed a total of sixty items. Apparently this was the extent of the itemization of the published budget. For administrative purposes, after approval, the budget was broken down into over fifteen hundred accounts. The Supreme Court of Utah held that the budget, as published, was sufficiently itemized to comply with the law.[28] From this case and similar ones, it appeared that very broad classifications in school budgets will be judicially sustained as complying with the itemization requirement.

Related to the itemization problem is the question of the legal right of a board to transfer funds among the several items of the budget after it has been approved and adopted. In many states the procedure for shifting funds among the various budgetary items is prescribed by a statute. In these states, of course, this procedure is a necessary condition of inter-budgetary changes. The statute in Arizona is illustrative. The following budgetary provision appears:

No expenditures shall be made for a purpose not particularly itemized and included in such budget, and no expenditure shall be made, and no debt, obligation or liability shall be incurred or created in any year for any purpose itemized in such budget in excess of the amount specified for such item. . . .

This statute was construed in a recent decision by the Supreme Court of Arizona. The heart of the question before the court was whether very broad classifications constituted sufficient itemization to state the "purpose" for which expenditures were to be made under the statutory provision quoted above.

As prepared, the budget consisted of six general categories. Among them were Administration and Instruction. A description of these two categories will be sufficient for this discussion. The various categories contained a number of sub-items. Sub-items under the general category of Administration, were superintendent, assistant superintendent, administrative officers, secretary and clerical assistants, and certain others. Under the general category of Instruction were such sub-items as principals, classroom teachers, other instructional personnel, librarians, and a number of others. The sub-items under the six general categories were forty-one in number. The question then arose as to the legal authority of the board to shift funds from one sub-item to another and from one general category to another. The court held that the board had authority to transfer funds among the various sub-items in each general category but not among the general categories themselves. To illustrate, under the general category Instruction, the board might transfer funds from sub-item principals to sub-item classroom teachers, but would not be entitled to transfer funds from sub-item principals under the general category Instruction to the sub-item salary of attendance officers under the general category Administration. The court explained its holding in the following language:

> It appears to us that to bind either the school district or the superintendent to a forty-one-line operating expense budget as advocated by the appellant would be impractical, unduly restrictive, and lead to absurd results. We, therefore, hold that the word "purpose", as used in the above sections, has reference . . . to the six general categories rather than the forty-one subitems contained therein. As a consequence the superintendent is authorized to draw warrants in excess of the amounts budgeted for subitems within any of the six general categories of the operating expense division so long as such will not exceed the total amount budgeted in the general category in which such subitems are included.[29]

The court was of the opinion that when a particular word, such as the word "purpose" as used in the statute quoted, is susceptible of more than one interpretation, that interpretation should be placed upon it which would appear to be reasonable and convenient. Certainly the court was not inclined to place a restrictive and narrow interpretation upon the statute in order unduly to restrict the exercise of the discretion of the board in the administration of the school budget.

In many jurisdictions the raising of money by taxation and the determination of certain budgetary expenditures for all governmental functions, including public education, is reposed in a single board. In Virginia, for example, that board is the board of supervisors. The question frequently arises whether such a body can modify the school budget presented to it by the school authorities. A case decided by the Supreme Court of Virginia will illustrate the nature of the controversy. The school budget in question contained many items, among them one for $2,700 for an increase in the salary of the superintendent of schools. The board of supervisors reduced the item to $2,000. After that amount had been spent for the purpose stated, the treasurer refused to honor further the warrants of the school board in payment of the superintendent's salary. The court was asked to determine whether the board of supervisors is authorized only to determine the total amount of local funds to be raised for schools, or may, in addition, determine the amounts of individual items of expenditure. The court stated that the obvious reason for the plan of taxation in use in Virginia is that one board can take a more comprehensive view of all local tax needs and fix a just and equitable tax rate. However, the court emphasized the fact that the board of supervisors is not charged with the "establishment, maintenance, and operation of the public school system." From the beginning the school boards in Virginia have had a separate corporate existence, and have been charged with the responsibility for maintaining and operating the public schools. The court held that the supervisors may determine only the total amount to be levied for school purposes and may not determine individual items of expenditure. It reasoned as follows:

> It would be illogical to make the School Board solely responsible for the efficient conduct of the school system, and then give another board control over the expenditures to be made by the School Board. . . . If the board of supervisors has control of the various items of the budget, it could

exercise a large amount of control over the operation of the school system, and there would be a serious division of authority, which it would not seem the legislature would have intended. . . .[30]

SCHOOL BOARD RECORDS

In General

School board records are very important legal documents, and should be kept and written with the same care and accuracy as other important documents. State statutes on the point are common and may be either mandatory or only directory. Normally if the statute provides that the board shall keep certain records it is likely that the courts will declare the statute mandatory, that is, the specified records must be kept and failure to keep them invalidates the board action not so recorded. On the other hand, if the statute is general, and provides only that the clerk shall keep a record of board proceedings, it probably would be declared to be directory only, and failure to record an action of the board would not invalidate the action.

Failure to keep adequate records under mandatory statutory provisions may result in substantial hardships to individuals. For example, in an Illinois case a teacher was "employed" but had received no written contract. However, a record of the board's vote to employ him appeared in the minutes, but not in the form and detail required by the Illinois statute on the point. The teacher sued the board for damages for breach of his contract. His suit was unsuccessful because of the defective nature of the record of the board's action by which the teacher was purportedly employed. The Illinois statute and the holding in this case appear in the following language of the Appellate Court of Illinois:

> . . . [The law] directs that the clerk shall keep . . . a record of the official acts of the board and that on all questions involving the expenditure of money, the yeas and nays shall be taken and entered on the records of the proceedings of the board. Such provisions are mandatory and failure to observe them is fatal. . . . The purpose of the statute requiring a yea and nay vote and the recording of the same is to give the taxpayers an opportunity to know how each member voted. The method followed by . . . [the board] gives no such information and is in direct violation of the statutory provisions.[31]

Occasions have arisen in which the personal liability of school authorities has depended on the completeness and accuracy with which records of board proceedings have been kept. For example, in Mississippi, a teacher brought an action for damages against board members individually and the superintendent of schools. The teacher alleged that she had been illegally discharged. The board's defense was that she had been issued no formal contract and this fact seems to have been established by the evidence. The law of Mississippi requires no written contract with teachers. The teacher had been notified of her employment. The supreme court of that state held that if the teacher could prove the facts she alleged, she was entitled to recover from the board members personally. She had alleged that her discharge had been wilful and malicious. The court stated that the law in Mississippi is that an order entered in board minutes is evidence of the acts of the board. It then held that the board owed the teacher a duty to enter the order of her employment in the minutes and that a failure to do so rendered the board members individually liable.[82] It stated specifically that the trustees had breached their duty to the teacher and became liable for such damages as flowed from such breach of duty to her. The importance of accurate and complete board minutes can, therefore, hardly be overemphasized.

Board Minutes as Public Documents

Unless statutes provide otherwise, it is the general rule that minutes of board meetings are public documents or writings and thus are open to inspection by the public. In some states certain documents are specifically designated as public in nature. It is important to call this fact to the attention of the secretary of the board, since he may be inclined to use greater care in the preparation of board minutes than might be expected if the secretary is unaware that the minutes he prepares may be subject to public scrutiny. Furthermore, knowledge of the fact that the records of board proceedings are public documents may have a salutary effect upon board action in that the board may be expected to exercise greater care if it is aware that a written record of the proceedings may freely be examined by the public.

In some instances it becomes important to determine the point at which the notes of the secretary taken at board meetings cease to be notes and actually become minutes and thus public documents. The Supreme

Court of Utah has considered this question. On the day following a board meeting certain persons asked permission to examine and copy the minutes of the meeting. The secretary denied the requesting parties permission to examine the notes. The court held that the secretary's untranscribed notes were not "public writings" under the statute, and thus were not required to be made available for public inspection. As the court states, the statutes and cases relating to public writings "are divergent as the shades of the spectrum." In other words, there appears to be no specific and infallible rule of thumb by which it may be determined when notes of board proceedings become minutes. The court said:

> . . . between two extremes, not necessarily midway, there is a point where reason shows brightest, dimming as the point shifts in one direction or the other. To hold that public writing includes the unexpurgated scribbled notes of a clerk, legible, perhaps to him alone, would be unreasonable, we think, and even might deify doodling. It would be unreasonable also to hold that any record made by a Clerk short of approval by a board and placement in a Journal, is not a public writing. Such conclusion might deify dawdling. We hold, therefore, that the Clerk's untranscribed notes reasonably are not classifiable as public writings . . . whereas the transcribed minutes, in final form, but awaiting only approval and placement in the Journal, are a public writing. . . .[33]

The court then addressed itself to the question of when board minutes should be available for public inspection. In the opinion of the court, they should be made available within a reasonable time. What constitutes a reasonable time may vary from case to case. Minutes of board actions of great importance to the public should be recorded and released in the shortest possible time. If the actions are not of such great importance, doubtless publication of the minutes may be delayed for a longer period. All that the law appears to require is that the board and the secretary act reasonably and in good faith in making board minutes available to the public. It seems clear that final approval of the minutes at a board meeting is not a condition to the right of the public to inspect them.

CITATIONS

1. McCormick v. Board of Education, 58 N.M. 648, 274 P.2d 299 (1954).
2. Montenegro-Riehm Music Co. v. Board of Education, 147 Ky. 720, 145 S.W. 740 (1912).

3. Kinney v. Howard, 133 Ia. 94, 110 N.W. 282 (1907).
4. Bowles v. Fayetteville Graded Schools, 211 N.C. 36, 188 S.E. 615 (1936).
5. Petition of Auditors of Hatfield Twp. School Dist., 161 Pa. Super. 388, 54 A.2d 833 (1947).
6. *In re* German Township School Directors, 46 D. & C. 562 (Pa. 1942).
7. Ready v. Board of Education, 297 Ill. App. 342, 17 N.E.2d 635 (1938).
8. Mullins v. Eveland, 234 S.W.2d 639 (Mo. App. 1950).
9. Keyes v. School District, 74 Idaho 314, 261 P.2d 811 (1953).
10. Russ v. Board of Education, 232 N.C. 1289, 59 S.E.2d 589 (1950).
11. Eastman v. School District, 120 Mont. 63, 180 P.2d 472 (1947).
12. Travis v. Teter, 370 Pa. 326, 87 A.2d 177 (1952).
13. Hudson v. Board of Education, 41 Ohio App. 402, 179 N.E. 701 (1931).
14. Board of Education v. Kennedy, 256 Ala. 478, 55 So.2d 511 (1951).
15. State *ex rel.* Rogers v. Board of Education, 125 W.Va. 579, 25 S.E.2d 537 (1947).
16. School District v. Thompson, 121 Colo. 275, 214 P.2d 1020 (1950).
17. Anthony v. School District, 55 Ariz. 265, 100 P.2d 988 (1944).
18. Laney v. Holbrook, 150 Fl. 622, 8 So.2d 465 (1942).
19. Mackler v. Board of Education, 16 N.J. 362, 108 A.2d 854 (1954)
20. Rehberg v. Board of Education, 345 Mich. 731, 77 N.W.2d 131 (1956).
21. Conley v. Board of Education, 143 Conn. 488, 123 A.2d 747 (1956).
22. Grady v. Marshall, 288 P.2d 1101 (Okla. 1955).
23. Kiner v. Well, 71 N.W.2d 743 (N.D. 1955).
24. State of Missouri v. Rone, 293 S.W.2d 1 (Mo. 1956).
25. Wann v. School District, 293 S.W.2d 408 (Mo. 1956).
26. State v. McGlynn, 135 N.E.2d 632 (Ohio 1956).
27. People v. Reilly Tar & Chemical Corp., 389 Ill. 434, 59 N.E.2d 843 (1945).
28. Tuttle v. Board of Education, 77 Utah 270, 294 P. 294 (1930).
29. Isley v. School Dist., 305 P.2d 432 (Ariz. 1956).
30. Board of Supervisors v. School Board, 182 Va. 266, 28 S.E.2d 698 (1944).
31. Ready v. Board of Education, 297 Ill. App. 342, 17 N.E.2d 635 (1938).
32. Stokes v. Newell, 174 Miss. 629, 165 So. 542 (1936).
33. Conover v. Board of Education, 1 Utah 2d 375, 267 P.2d 768 (1954).

X

LIABILITY OF SCHOOL DISTRICTS
AND BOARD MEMBERS

Often it is difficult or impossible to understand the problem of the liability of school board members except in the light of district liability. In some situations, in some states, both the district and board members may be held liable for their acts. Under other circumstances, only board members, only the district, or neither, may be held. Since the liability of board members and the liability of districts are determined by the application of quite different legal principles, they will be considered separately.

LIABILITY OF DISTRICTS

Contracts

In most states, school districts are designated corporations by express provision of statute. Since they are statutory creatures, they have only the powers granted them by the law and certain limited implied powers. This point is treated in Chapter I. Ordinarily statutes expressly confer upon districts the authority to contract, but even in the absence of statutes, some contractual powers would be implied. However, as indicated in Chapter VII, districts do not have the unlimited authority to contract usually possessed by individuals. In that chapter it was also observed that under certain limited conditions, districts, through their boards, may be required to pay the reasonable value of goods or services even though the board actually may have exceeded its contractual authority. It might be helpful to review that discussion in this connection.

Torts

A tort is defined as a wrong, private or civil in nature, which does not flow from the breach of a contract. For example, trespassing upon the property of another, performing negligent acts which cause injury to another, illegally striking another person, and similar acts are torts. The torts with which we will be primarily concerned in this discussion are those in which it was sought to hold the school district liable for the negligent or other wrongful acts of district officers or employees.

The legal rule under the common law is that districts are not liable for damages caused by the negligent acts of their officers or employees. The three states of California, New York, and Washington, however, impose tort liability directly upon school districts. Connecticut, New Jersey, and New York on statewide bases and Wyoming on a local option basis have statutes which make school districts financially responsible for the negligence of their employees while the employees are acting within the scope of their employment; that is, districts must pay any judgments for damages obtained against employees for wrongful acts of employees in the line of duty. This type of statute is often called a "save harmless" statute because it "saves" district employees from financial "harm" by making the district indemnify them. These laws permit school districts to insure themselves for this purpose. The statutes of Connecticut and New Jersey expressly cover board members under the same conditions as employees. All other states, with a few minor exceptions, adhere to the rule that districts are immune from tort liability. The foundation of the immunity rule is most frequently said by the courts to be the principle that a state cannot be sued without its consent, and since school districts are arms or agencies of the state, the immunity of the state from suit extends to school districts. Some courts say that the doctrine stems from the old rule that "the King can do no wrong." Still others deny liability on the ground that no funds are available from which to pay any tort judgment which may be had against school districts without depleting funds necessary to maintain the schools.

Although the doctrine is a judicial creation, it has not been uniformly popular among legal authorities. Judge Latimer, of the Supreme Court of Utah, expressed a not unusual judicial attitude on the rule as follows:

> While the law writers, editors and judges have criticized and disapproved the foregoing doctrine of governmental immunity as illogical and unjust,

the weight of precedent of decided cases supports the general rule and we prefer not to disregard a principle so well established without statutory authority. We, therefore, adopt the rule of the majority and hold that school boards cannot be held liable for ordinary negligent acts.[1]

Although the immunity doctrine is well established, it is subject to well recognized exceptions. One is that a district is liable for torts if it engages in "proprietary" functions as distinguished from "governmental" ones. The line of demarcation between the two types of functions is far from distinct and some courts have declined to try to draw it. A second exception is that school districts may be held liable if they maintain nuisances. A large number of suits have been brought against districts in which it has been sought to bring the cases within one of the recognized exceptions to the immunity rule. These efforts are occasionally successful. Among the suits which have been successful is one which arose in Arizona. Two school districts had rented the stadium of the Tucson district for a football game. Because of a defect in a railing of the stadium, a spectator fell and was seriously injured. He brought an action, not against the schools whose teams were playing, but against the Tucson district, the owner of the stadium. The rule of immunity of school districts is followed in Arizona. The question then is whether the Tucson district, by renting its stadium to the two districts and charging a rental therefor, had abandoned its "governmental" function and embarked upon a "proprietary" one, thereby becoming liable under an exception to the immunity rule. The Supreme Court of Arizona agreed with the plaintiff that the district was engaging in a proprietary function, and rendered judgment in his favor against the district.[2]

There are statements by courts which indicate that the distinction between governmental and proprietary functions is sometimes adopted for the express purpose of decreasing the severity of the immunity rule. A statement by Judge Erickson of the Supreme Court of Montana in a dissenting opinion is an example. He said:

> Most of the states, in attempting to decrease the severity of the rule [i.e. the rule of immunity], have adopted the governmental-proprietary test. The test is an arbitrary one, but the general trend of the decisions is to declare more and more functions proprietary rather than governmental so as to allow recovery. It is now generally agreed that neither logic nor justice supports the general rule which in this case denies recovery to the person injured as in this case where she goes for entertainment to a

basketball game sponsored by the school district, while on the other hand for exactly the same injury under the same conditions she could recover if she had gone to a theater and had been there injured.[3]

It has become rather common for persons injured as a result of failure of boards to maintain school premises in a safe condition, to base their suits upon the exception which permits recovery against districts if they maintain nuisances. The difficulty of determining what constitutes a nuisance has been recognized by many courts, and some of them have refused to recognize exceptions because of this difficulty. It has been held, for example, that discharging sewage into a stream, maintaining a defective privy well on school property, and maintaining a flagpole in an unsafe condition are nuisances for which districts may be held liable. There is even disagreement as to whether maintaining a flagpole in an unsafe condition constitutes a nuisance. On the other hand, an unfumigated schoolroom in which a tubercular teacher had taught was held not to be an actionable nuisance.

The Supreme Court of Tennessee is among the courts which, in regard to district liability, refuse to recognize the distinction between the maintenance of nuisances by districts and other torts committed by districts. In a recent case, it appeared that a child had been injured by falling into a concrete stairway leading from the playground to the basement of the school building. The stair opening had been partially barricaded by defective iron pipes, leaving the opening unprotected A little boy was thrown through the unprotected opening, and fell fourteen feet to the bottom of the concrete stairway He suffered serious and permanent injuries, and sought to recover damages on the ground that an unprotected stairway was a nuisance maintained by the district. Suit on behalf of the child failed. The court held that the district was not liable.[4] The court did not decide whether maintaining the stairway in an unsafe condition constituted a nuisance. It was not necessary for it to do so since it held that the immunity rule extends even to nuisances in Tennessee.

In the Kansas City, Kansas, school district, a large circular wash basin had been constructed in the basement of one of the schools for the use of third grade children. The children splashed water on the floor while using the basin, and threw wet paper towels on the floor, rendering the floor very slippery. A nine-year-old girl slipped and fell on the floor and was severely injured. The general rule of district immunity is followed in Kansas, hence the injured girl sought to bring her case under the nuisance exception. The girl's suit was unsuccessful. The Supreme Court of Kansas held that a wash basin located in a school building is not a nuisance even though failure to maintain it properly might cause injury to pupils.[5]

There are many judicial definitions of nuisance. Perhaps the one stated by the Supreme Court of Connecticut is as accurate as any. According to that court:

> In its proper use . . . [the word "nuisance"] involves as an essential element that it can be the natural tendency of the act or thing complained of to create danger and inflict injury upon person or property.[6]

Despite the breadth of this and other similar definitions of nuisance, it is quite impossible to determine what unsafe conditions will be categorized by the courts as nuisances. There appears to be little or no agreement among the courts on the question.

Liability Insurance

It will be recalled that one of the reasons assigned in support of the district tort immunity rule is that there are no funds from which a judgment against a district can be paid—that the use of district funds to pay a tort judgment might result in such dissipation of district funds as to disable the district from carrying on essential school functions. The question then arises whether the immunity rule should apply if the district legally carries liability insurance from which a tort judgment may be paid without disturbing school funds. This problem has been considered very thoroughly by the courts of Illinois. In a leading case on the point, a child was injured while playing on the playground, it being charged that the negligence of the teachers resulted in the loss of an eye to the child. It was alleged on behalf of the child that the district carried liability insurance in an amount sufficient to pay any judgment the child might recover against the district. In a suit against the district for damages, the district set up the usual defense that it was not liable for the negligent act of its agents, that is, the teachers. The suit by the child was successful. The Appellate Court of Illinois, Third District, was of the opinion that since the school funds were protected, the basic reason for the immunity rule ceases to exist. The court quoted the following language from an earlier decision of the Supreme Court of Illinois:

"We are of the opinion there is no justification for absolute immunity if the trust is protected because that has been the reason for the rule of absolute immunity. Reason and justice require an extension of the rule in an attempt to inject some humanitarian principles into the abstract rule of absolute immunity. The law is not static and must follow and conform to changing conditions and new trends in human relations to justify its existence as a servant and protector of the people, and when necessary new remedies must be applied where none exist." [7]

From this reasoning it seems to follow that suits against districts for damages caused by the negligent acts of its officers or employees may succeed if, in the payment of a judgment which may be obtained, recourse may be had to the proceeds of insurance policies, so that it is not necessary to use public funds to pay it. Legality of purchase of liability insurance by school districts is treated in Chapter VI.

Independent Contractors

In those states in which liability is imposed upon districts for their torts, they may sometimes escape liability through the employment of independent contractors, instead of servants and employees. Independent contractors are distinguished from servants and employees mainly in that they are subject to the employer's control only in the results of the work to be accomplished, but are not subject to control of the employer as to the ways and means of performing the work. Servants and employees are subject to detailed direction of their employers. However, districts may not escape liability in all cases through the employment of independent contractors. If districts are liable at all, there are imposed upon them certain obligations which cannot be delegated to independent contractors. For example, if there rests upon the district the obligation to keep its premises safe, districts may not avoid this liability through the device of employing independent contractors to perform the work. The trend appears to be toward fewer responsibilities which may be avoided by districts through the employment of independent contractors.

LIABILITY OF BOARD MEMBERS

Illegal School Contracts

Public education is big business, and the larger it becomes the more opportunities are afforded for boards of education, in the management of the schools, to become involved in legal problems. It must be borne in mind that school boards generally are elected by popular vote, and that often their members have not had the advantage of extensive business training and experience. Even more frequently, they are persons without legal training. Thus it is not surprising that boards consisting principally of laymen, when charged with the responsibility of managing school business, often involving very large sums of money, may sometimes violate the law. Violations may result from mere mistakes of judgment, from misunderstanding of the law, or, unhappily, from attempts to reap personal advantage and profit through the abuse of discretion with which board members are clothed by the law.

Individuals, as distinguished from governmental agencies, are bound at their peril to know the limits which may exist as to their authority. For example, if an agent represents himself as having authority to bind the individual for whom he purports to act, and it subsequently develops that the agent had no such authority, the agent is liable to the third party with whom he has dealt. The liability of the agent rests upon what the law refers to as breach of an implied warranty that the agent had the authority to act for the principal in question.

Members of school boards, however, are not held to the same extent of knowledge as to the scope of their authority as the agent purporting to act for an individual or company. Rather, if school board members act in good faith, without fraud, they will not generally be held personally liable if it subsequently develops that their actions were not, in fact, legally authorized. It has frequently been said by the courts that those who deal with boards of education are legally bound to know the limit on boards' authority. Those who deal with boards of education are in as good a position to know the legal limitations on the boards' power as are the boards themselves. It follows, therefore, that persons dealing with boards may not cast upon the boards the responsibility of knowing or determining the extent to which the contractual authority of boards is limited by law. Boards of education are charged by law with the administration of school systems, which administration is subject to regulation by a wide variety of complicated laws which frequently are not completely understood by able lawyers and judges. Much less should lay boards be held to understand in detail the laws to which their actions are subject. It has been stated by some courts that if individual members of school boards are to be held personally liable for their illegal acts resulting from mistakes of judgment, persons of financial responsibility would be extremely reluctant to accept membership on boards of education. Educational policies would then be placed principally, if not entirely, in the hands of boards made up of members who would be financially unable to pay a judgment. Obviously, however, public interest demands that board membership not be limited in this way.

Despite the legal protection afforded members of school boards, they are not immune from legal liability personally for any and all acts they may perform contrary to law. All public officers, including school board members, are liable for their wrongful acts if their acts are actuated by malice, or result from willfulness or other intentional and deliberate wrongdoing. Comparison of representative cases will indicate the judicial attitude and approach to problems in this area. In Texas, a certain teacher had been employed conditional upon the meeting of stated requirements. A board, in good faith, decided that the teacher in question did not meet the requirements, discharged her, and employed another in her place. However, after a hearing, the State Superintendent of Public Instruction ruled that the teacher had a valid contract and that the board was legally obligated to pay her salary in full for the year. The matter finally reached the Supreme Court of Texas. There was no allegation that the action of the board was actuated by malice or that it was guilty of any intentional wrongdoing in discharging the teacher. It was guilty of nothing more than mistaken judgment. There would clearly be an action against the district for the teacher's salary, but a judgment against the district would avail her nothing since the funds of the district for the school year covered by her contract were exhausted. Her only practical recourse was to try to recover from the members of the board personally. The court refused to hold the board members personally liable. It said:

> To hold . . . [the board members] personally liable when they were guilty of no wrong whatsoever, but in good faith were trying to comply with what reasonably appeared to be the then rulings of the State Superintendent, would be to impose upon public officials charged with discretionary duties personal liability for mistaken judgment. We cannot assent to that doctrine.[8]

The court recognized the regrettable injustice to the teacher, but said that no blame for that situation could be visited upon the trustees, who, in good faith, exercised their best judgment in the matter.

In a case which arose in Mississippi, it appeared that the school board had sought to abrogate a teacher's contract which had been entered into by a board, some of the membership of which had changed at a subsequent election. In her suit against the board members, both individually and in their official capacity, she alleged that she had been discharged "wrongfully and without legal right, and arbitrarily, for purely personal and political motives." The Supreme Court of Mississippi sustained the validity of the teacher's contract. On the question of the individual liability of board members the court stated the rule in the following language:

> It is true that officers are not liable for the honest exercise of discretionary powers confided to them, but when they go outside their powers and commit wrongs under the color of office, there is liability. They are not given immunity from willful wrongs or malicious acts.[9]

Torts

The immunity from tort liability which school districts enjoy does not extend to district employees. Drivers of school buses, laboratory supervisors, coaches and instructors in physical education courses, and, indeed, all other district employees, are as liable to pay damages caused by their wrongful acts as if they were employees of a private organization or individual. However, such liability does not extend to school board members since they are not employees of the district. Rather they are officers of the state, and are subject to an entirely different rule of liability than the rule applied to district employees. The rule applicable to them is that they are not liable for damages which may result from their honest exercise of discretion within their express or implied powers as school officers. Of course, there is the familiar requirement that the acts of school officers must not be corrupt or malicious if they are to escape liability for damages which their acts may have caused.

This rule was applied and discussed by the Supreme Court of North Carolina. In the case before the court, it appeared that certain repairs were being made on the school stadium. Under the direction of members of the board, cement blocks had been hauled to the stadium and stacked where the board members had directed. According to the complaint, the blocks were stacked on a hillside adjacent to a cement wall which had been erected around the stadium. At a game held at the park, a spectator was seated near the pile of blocks which fell against the cement wall and crushed it to the ground. The wall and blocks fell upon the spectator, injuring him so seriously that he died a short time thereafter. Since the immunity rule protects districts from liability in North Carolina in such cases, the only recourse, if any, for damages which the estate of the deceased had would be against the individual members of the school board. They were, therefore, made parties to the suit. The court, in denying liability against the individual members, stated:

> It is settled law in this jurisdiction that a public official, engaged in the performance of governmental duties involving the exercise of judgment and discretion, may not be held personally liable for mere negligence in respect thereto. The rule in such cases is that an official may not be held liable unless it be alleged and proved that his act, or failure to act, was corrupt or malicious, . . . or that he acted outside of and beyond the scope of his duties. . . . And, while an employee of an agency of government, as distinguished from a public official, is generally held individually liable for negligence in the performance of his duties, nevertheless such negligence may not be imputed to the employer . . . when such employer is clothed with governmental immunity. . . .
>
> In the instant case the School Trustees and Park Commissioners were engaged in official, administrative acts involving the exercise of discretion at the times laid in the complaint. It is not alleged that their conduct was either corrupt or malicious. Nor does it appear that they were acting beyond the scope of their duties as such trustees or commissioners. Under the modern concept of public education, which recognizes the necessity of ministering to the physical as well as the mental needs of school children, an athletic field for games and exhibitions, with grandstand and other seating facility, is an essential part of the physical plant of a well integrated school unit. This being so, the action of the School Trustees and Park Commissioners in providing for the erection of a grandstand may not be treated as an activity beyond the scope of their duties as such public officials.[10]

There are cases in which board members have been held personally liable in tort when they have failed to carry out ministerial, as distinguished from discretionary, duties. The distinction between the two types of duties is not always clearly discernible. The Supreme Court of Indiana attempted the distinction in a case similar to the one in North Carolina which we have just discussed. Here the school board each year conducted a "Field Day Exhibition." Temporary stands were constructed in which spectators were seated. The board employed a carpenter to build the stands under the direction of the clerk of the board. Because of defective construction the seats fell and caused serious injury to a number of spectators. Since the district immunity rule is followed in Indiana, one of the injured persons sued the individual board members for damages.

The members advanced the usual defense that they were not individually liable for mistakes made in the performance of their duties which involved the exercise of discretion. The defense did not prevail and the board members were held individually liable. According to the court, a duty is discretionary "when it involves on the part of the officer to determine whether he should perform a certain act, and, if so, in what particular way." However, the performance of *ministerial* acts in implementing the discretionary decision does not fall within the definition, and board members are not protected from personal liability in the negligent performance of ministerial acts. The court distinguished between the two types of board acts in the following language:

> . . . we hold that the appellees, members of the school board, in determining that there should be field day exercises, in connection with their school, were acting within their jurisdiction, and that such act, together with their action in determining the manner in which such exercises should be conducted was discretionary, and that for injuries resulting therefrom they were not liable, but that the duties performed in making preparation for such field day exercises and the general management thereof were ministerial acts, for the negligent performance of which, if so performed, whether performed by themselves, by their agent, or by an independent contractor, they were liable for damages for injuries suffered by reason thereof.[11]

Failure to Obey Express Statutes

Board members have been held personally liable when they have refused or failed to follow specific statutory procedures. When the law requires boards to follow designated procedures, no discretion in the matter is left to the boards. Therefore, when it appears that boards have intentionally or negligently deviated from statutory procedure, they have been held personally liable. Such liability may be imposed upon them by statute, or may flow from the general rule of liability.

Pennsylvania imposes criminal liability upon board members under the circumstances just described by express statutory provision. The law on this point has been construed by the Superior Court of Pennsylvania in a case which well represents the judicial attitude on this question. The statute involved was the familiar one requiring that contracts involving expenditures in excess of a stated amount be let to the lowest responsible bidder. The law provided that exceptions may be made in cases of emergency, but no emergency appeared in this case. It appeared that although the board had held a number of meetings in which it might well have considered letting the contract for certain school painting jobs to the lowest responsible bidder, it was alleged that the board members willfully refused and failed to obey a positive statutory duty by purchasing supplies without competitive bidding. According to the court, they had willfully breached a positive statutory duty of a ministerial nature, and were held guilty.[12]

In Kentucky, the members of a school board were held individually liable as a result of their failure to procure school bus insurance as the law requires. The statute involved is as follows:

> Each board of education may set aside funds to provide for . . . insurance against the negligence of drivers or operators of school buses owned or operated by the board. If the transportation of pupils is let out under contract, the contract shall require the contractor to carry . . . insurance against negligence in such amounts as the board designates. In either case the . . . policy . . . shall bind the company to pay any final judgment rendered against the insured [district] for . . . damage to the property of any school child or death or injury of any school child or other person.

It will be observed that under this statute board members are *required* to demand that the contractor to whom the board lets contracts to transport pupils, procure insurance against injury caused by the contractor's negligent acts in operating the school bus. In other words, it is made mandatory upon the board to require the contractors to carry insurance to protect school children "or other persons" who might be injured. The board failed to require the bus contractor to procure the insurance as the law demands. The contractor, through his negligence in operating the bus, became involved in an accident in which a woman was killed. While the woman's estate had a valid action against the contractor and the driver of the bus, it is possible that these latter were not financially able to pay a judgment which might be rendered against them. Since there was no insurance carried on the bus, the estate clearly had no suit against an insurance company. The only recourse, therefore, was against the individual members of the school board for their failure to require the contractor to purchase insurance as they were required by the law to do. The Court of Appeals of Kentucky held the board members individually liable. It stated that the duty of the board to require bus drivers with whom it contracts to carry liability insurance is a specific and definite one. It emphasized that the board had no discretion in the matter. The duty was mandatory. It stated that for the failure to carry out the specific mandates of the legislature, board members are individually liable for loss which flows from that failure.[18]

Illegal Expenditure of School Funds

In the disbursement of school funds, it is impossible to avoid occasional irregular or illegal expenditures. Heretofore we have found that boards are not bound at their peril to determine the legality of their acts in all cases. However, there are certain circumstances under which board members may be compelled personally to restore to the district money illegally expended. The courts consistently point out two types of illegal expenditures. The first type are those which are expressly prohibited by statutory or constitutional provision. In other words, expenditures so prohibited are completely beyond the power of the board and are complete nullities. For this type of illegal expenditures board members are bound to answer personally. A case which arose in Nebraska will illustrate this type. At a regular meeting of the board a resolution was passed to provide a home for the superintendent, for a sum which was not to exceed $2,500. The board purchased land upon which to construct the proposed residence and paid for it out of the funds of the district. Certain taxpayers sued to have the transaction nullified, and to require the individual members of the board to pay out of their personal funds the sum of $2,500 which it was alleged had been illegally expended.

The Supreme Court of Nebraska held that under the law of that state the construction of a superintendent's home at the expense of the district was completely beyond the power of the board, and its action was declared to be ultra vires. Since this expenditure was not legal under any circumstances, the board members were held individually liable.[14]

Another very important point was decided in the Nebraska case just discussed. Although a majority of the members of the board voted to spend district money for the illegal construction, two members of the board voted against the expenditure. In imposing personal liability upon individual board members, the court excluded from liability those members who voted against the expenditure. In other words, it was determined that a majority vote of a board to approve an illegal act of the district, does not bind personally those members of the board who vote against the illegal action.

The second type of illegal expenditure to which the courts refer is one which is within the power of boards to make, but which is illegal only because the manner and form of making it have not been in accordance with legal requirements. For example, a board may be authorized to make certain expenditures, and the law may specify that the expenditures be authorized by a roll-call vote of the board at a regular board meeting. A roll-call vote affects only the manner of authorizing the expenditure and not the power of the board to make it. If it appears that the board acted in good faith and violated the law as to the particular expenditures only in that they were made in an irregular manner, the members of the board will not be held personally liable therefor.

Illegal Suspension or Expulsion of Pupils

The right of pupils to attend school has been uniformly held to be a valuable one which the law will protect. It follows that if a pupil has been illegally suspended or expelled from school, he may bring a mandamus action to compel the board to readmit him. If the suspension or expulsion has not yet occurred, but is threatened, an injunction may be obtained forbidding school authorities to carry out the threatened illegal act.

As to the personal liability of board members for illegal exclusion of pupils from school, the rule is that individual board members are not liable for mere mistakes in judgment in suspending or expelling pupils. However, they are individually liable if it can be shown that their act was willful and malicious. Also, of course, they may be held personally liable for violation of any express statute on expulsion or suspension.

Although the problem seems to have arisen infrequently, there is a possibility that, under certain circumstances, board members may be held individually liable for injury to the feelings of a pupil if he is illegally expelled from school. An early Massachusetts case suggests the possibility that such damages may be recovered. Among other things, the pupil asked the court to instruct the jury that in a suit against the City of Lawrence for his illegal expulsion from school, injury to his feelings might be considered an element of damage. The Supreme Judicial Court of Massachusetts held that injury to his feelings or his standing in the community may properly be taken into account in determining the pupil's damages for wrongful expulsion.[15]

Removal of Board Members from Office

Not only may members of school boards be required to respond personally in damages in certain cases, but they may also be removed from office for official wrongdoing. In many states, the statutes specify the grounds upon which public officers, including school board members, may be removed. Of course, it does not follow that an official guilty of misfeasance or malfeasance in office may not be removed in the absence of an express statute permitting his removal.

Official wrongdoing ranges from innocent mistakes to fraudulent and corrupt attempts by board members to gain a benefit at the expense of the district. It is not always easy to determine in advance of a judicial ruling whether the facts in a particular case will be held to constitute corrupt official action. For example, in Utah, the question arose whether a board member, after he had received all the salary allowed him by law, was guilty of a corrupt practice because he presented claims for additional amounts. The evidence showed that the board member involved did not know that he was making illegal charges. Under these circumstances, the Supreme Court of Utah held that his conduct did not constitute "malfeasance in office." The court said:

> We therefore come to the conclusion, in order to show that an officer who put in a claim for something which he was not entitled to or which the law did not authorize, generally called an illegal claim, that he must have done so knowing that he was doing wrong or at least under such circumstances that any reasonable person who had done the same thing would have known that he was doing something wrong. The innocent filing of an illegal claim, thinking he is entitled to it, does not make malfeasance in office in that regard.[16]

A number of courts have had occasion to consider the question whether board members may be removed from office for violation of the common statutory provision that board members may not have a direct or indirect financial interest in a school contract. This has arisen in California. The school law of that state contains the usual provision against a board member having such an interest. It appears that the Los Angeles School District contracted with a certain transportation company to transport pupils to and from the city schools. One member of the board was an insurance broker who wrote the insurance for the transportation company, and received his commission. The District Court of Appeal of California held that the board member may not legally participate in the insurance premiums paid by the transportation company. There was then presented against the board member an accusation that he had been guilty of "willful and corrupt misconduct in office," which is a statutory ground for removal of public officers in California. The board member insisted that he had acted in good faith and that his lawyer had informed him that his actions were not illegal. The evidence disclosed, however, that the board member may not have informed his lawyer of all of the facts in the case! The removal of the board member was sustained on the ground that he had been guilty of "willful and corrupt misconduct in office." Under the California law the phrase "willful and corrupt" is rather broad. On this point the court said:

> However, the phrase "willful or corrupt misconduct in office" does not necessarily imply corruption or criminal intention. It means "simply a purpose or willingness to commit the act,"—" a wrongful design to acquire or cause some pecuniary or other advantage to the person guilty of the act." [17]

Among the legal devices commonly employed to remove faithless officials from office is the recall election. As the name indicates, under this procedure the voters may vote an official out of office. This device was discussed and described by the Supreme Court of Michigan in a case in point. Recall was initiated by the usual method of filing a petition by a specified number of electors requesting the board to call a recall election. The board declined to call it and the appropriate action was brought to compel it to do so. The petition, signed by the requisite number of voters, set out, as reasons for removing the board member in question, a number of his alleged official wrongdoings. Among the alleged reasons were the board member's failure to require competitive bids on certain contracts, the use of the school station wagon for his personal purposes, and his receipt of wages from the district in violation of law. The Supreme Court of Michigan held that at least some of the reasons specified in the petition were sufficiently definite to support the petition for a recall, and ordered the board to call a recall election.[18] In describing the petition, the court stated that a petition for recall does not require the exact technical proof required in proceedings for removal. In the petition for recall, the allegations need only be sufficient to bring the recall matter before the people for action. The petition itself need furnish only sufficient information to the electors to enable them to form a judgment when called upon to vote. Whether the matters alleged are sufficient to justify removal is a question to be determined by the people at the ballot box.

CITATIONS

1. Bingham v. Board of Education., 118 Utah 582, 223 P.2d 432 (1950).
2. Sawaya v. Tucson High School Dist., 78 Ariz. 389, 281 P.2d 105 (1955).
3. Rhoads v. School Dist. No. 7, 115 Mont. 352, 142 P.2d 890 (1943).
4. Barnett v. City of Memphis, 196 Tenn. 590, 269 S.W.2d 906 (1954).
5. Jones v. Kansas City, 176 Kan. 406, 271 P.2d 803 (1954).
6. Laspino v. City of New Haven, 135 Conn. 603, 67 A.2d 557 (1949).
7. Thomas v. Broadlands Community Consol. School Dist., 348 Ill. App. 567, 109 N.E.2d 636 (1952).
8. Campbell v. Jones, 264 S.W.2d 425 (Tex. 1954).
9. Stokes v. Newell, 174 Miss. 629, 165 So. 542 (1936).
10. Smith v. Hefner, 235 N.C. 1, 68 S.E.2d 783 (1952).
11. Adams v. Schneider, 71 Ind. App. 249, 124 N.E. 718 (1919).
12. Commonwealth v. Zang, 142 Pa. Super. 566, 16 A.2d 741 (1940).
13. Bronaugh v. Murray, 294 Ky. 715, 172 S.W.2d 591 (1943).
14. Fulk v. School Dist. No. 8, 155 Neb. 630, 53 N.W.2d 57 (1952).
15. Morrison v. City of Lawrence, 181 Mass. 127, 63 N.E. 400 (1902).
16. Atwood v. Cox, 88 Utah 437, 55 P.2d 377 (1936).
17. People v. Becker, 112 Cal. App. 2d 324, 246 P.2d 103 (1952).
18. Eaton v. Baker, 334 Mich. 521, 55 N.W.2d 77 (1952).

INDEX

School elections. *See* Elections
School funds
  activity funds, 150-152
  budgets, 169-173
  disbursement, 150-152
  illegal expenditure, 189-190
  in general, 87
  raised locally, 3
  transfers of, 169, 170-172
  uses
    in general, 87-88
    insurance, 91-93
    miscellaneous, 93-94
    supplies and equipment, 88-89
    transportation, 89-91
  See also Contracts, Fees, and Liability
School property
  conduct on, 19-21
  giving away, 84
  in general, 76-78
  insurance, 91
  purchase, 93
  renting, 83-84, 179
  selling, 84, 149-150
  uses
    community, 78-81
    conflicting with businesses, 84-85
    political, 81-82
    religious, 41, 82-83
  See also Contracts and Liability
Secret societies, 21, 22, 24
Sectarian influences. *See* Church-state issues
Selling
  food, 85
  school property, 84
  supplies, 85
Sex differentials, 54-55
Sick leave, 60-61
Sites, 93, 149
Social security, 58
State and education, 2-3. *See also* Church-state issues and specific items
Strikes. *See* Collective bargaining
Students. *See* Pupil personnel
Studies. *See* Curriculum
Subjects. *See* Curriculum
Subversive influences
  books, 39-40
  curriculum, 32-33
  property, 79-82
  teachers, 68, 69, 70-73
  See also Communism, Loyalty of teachers, and Patriotism

Supplies, 85, 88-89. *See also* Bids and Contracts
Supreme Court of the United States
  Bible-reading, 40-41
  compulsory attendance, 9
  flag salute, 42
  home instruction, 11
  investigating committees, 72-73
  language teaching, 32
  loyalty law, 72
  loyalty oath, 71-72
  racial segregation, 18
  "released time," 41-42
  religious instruction, 41
  retirement, 59
  salary, 55-56
  secret societies, 21
  tenure, 55-56, 66-67
  textbooks, 89
  transportation, 90
  use of property, 80
  vaccination, 14-15
Suspension. *See* Conduct of pupils

Taxes. *See* School funds
Teachers. *See* Employed personnel
Tenure
  abolishing, 66-67
  and salary, 55-56, 66
  dismissal causes, 67-70
  elements of, 65-66
  hearings, 155-163
Textbooks
  damage to, 20
  in general, 39-40
  non-public schools, 89
Torts, 178-182, 185-187
Transfer of teachers, 53
Transportation
  in general, 89-91, 93-94
  limitations, 90-91
  of teachers, 56
  to non-public schools, 90

Un-American influences. *See* Subversive influences
Unions, 49-50, 62-64
Unprofessional conduct, 69, 70

Vacancies, school board, 128-131
  filling of, 131-132
Vaccination, 14-15
Voting, 152-155, 190. *See also* Elections

Workmen's compensation, 93